Let's Write Japanese in Japanese

Second Edition

[Hiragana]

Kimihiko Nomura
California State University, Chico

McGraw-Hill, Inc.
College Custom Series

New York St. Louis San Francisco Auckland **Bogotá**
Caracas Lisbon London Madrid Mexico Milan Montreal
New Delhi Paris San Juan Singapore Sydney Tokyo Toronto

McGraw-Hill's College Custom Series consists of products that are produced from camera-ready copy. Peer review, class testing, and accuracy are primarily the responsibility of the author(s).

This is a workbook with video instruction. For further information on the video, call McGraw-Hill, Inc. at (209) 276-0926.

LET'S WRITE JAPANESE IN JAPANESE

Copyright © 1994 by McGraw-Hill, Inc. All rights reserved. Printed in the United States of America. Except as permitted under the United States Copyright Act of 1976, no part of this publication may be reproduced or distributed in any form or by any means, or stored in a data base retrieval system, without prior written permission of the publisher.

1 2 3 4 5 6 7 8 9 0   9 0 9 8 7 6 5 4

ISBN 0-07-047075-8

Editor: Todd Bull

Cover Design: David M. Daly

PREFACE

Students of the Japanese Language should write in Japanese characters. In fact, it is mandatory for them to learn that Japanese is written in characters unrelated to English and other languages and to master these characters. Japanese documents are always written with Japanese characters. Hence, the students who study Japanese with Roma-ji (Roman) characters cannot read Japanese as it is written.

Responding to this frustrating problem faced by students of the language, this workbook of Hiragana characters, along with a second volume on Katakana characters, has been developed for English-speaking students of Japanese.

There are two volumes in this workbook series. Volume one focuses on Hiragana, and volume two focuses on Katakana. Both Hiragana and Katakana are Japanese phonetical symbols used in Japanese documents (together with Kan-ji, Chinese ideographics). Roma-ji is only supplemental in Japanese writing. Hence, as mentioned above, knowing Roma-ji does not give the student an ability to read or write Japanese.

Supplementing these workbooks are two volumes of videotapes. Each contains complete instruction on the stroke order, pronunciation, and usage of some special characters, plus student exercises.

These workbooks, together with the accompanying video instructions, may be used by Japanese-language teachers for instruction in the language or by students for self-study. Although these workbooks are suitable for use with any Japanese language textbook, it is highly recommended that they be used with the *Nhon-go Hyaku-ichi-ban* series by the author. This is because other textbooks available on the market often employ Roma-ji, and by the time Kana (both Japanese phonetical symbols) are introduced to the students, many have already acquired mispronunciations and incorrect writing habits in Japanese. Hence, they need to unlearn what they have already learned, an obvious waste of time and effort.

To maximize the efficiency of the time spent by the students in the acquisition of correct Japanese writing, each volume contains a variety of learning activities. For details on these activities, read the section "How to Use This Workbook" that follows.

My personal thanks are extended to Mr. Sam Sykes, instructional specialist in foreign languages for the Newport News Public School System, to Mr. Nick Koltun, media services director at Christopher Newport College, and to Mrs. Haku-u Takenoya, calligraphy instructor, Federation of Japanese Calligraphy Association, for their help in carrying out this project.

Kimihiko Nomura

TABLE OF CONTENTS

PREFACE	ii
HOW TO USE THIS WORKBOOK	1
Organization	1
On the Video	1
In the Workbook	2
Pronunciation Practice	2
Notes on Usage and Pronunciation	2
Stroke Practice Sheet	2
I. Trace	
II. Writing with quadrants	
III. Writing with and without quadrants	
IV. Writing without quadrants	
V. Free-standing	
Recognition and Dictation Exercise	3
PART I: 46 BASIC HIRAGANA CHARACTERS	4
Chart of 46 Basic Hiragana Characters	5
Notes on Usage and Pronunciation	6
Stroke Practice Sheets	8
Exercises	54
PART II: 25 HIRAGANA CHARACTERS WITH CONSONANTS:	
[g, z, d, j, b, p]	56
Chart of 25 Hiragana Characters	
with Consonants: [g, z, d, j, b, p]	57
Notes on Usage and Pronunciation	57
Stroke Practice Sheets	58
Exercises	71
PART IIII: 36 HIRAGANA CHARACTERS WITH SEMI-VOWEL: [y]	73
Chart of 36 Hiragana Characters	
with Semi-vowel: [y]	74
Notes on Usage and Pronunciation	75
Stroke Practice Sheets	76
Exercises	93
APPENDICES	95
APPENDIX A List of Exercise Answers	96
APPENDIX B List of Vocabulary Words	98
APPENDIX C List of All Hiragana Characters	100

How to Use This Workbook

This workbook is designed solely for use with the video cassette tape, which demonstrates the correct stroke order and pronunciation of Hiragana. Hence, it is essential that you acquire the videotape and practice the strokes and pronunciation of Hiragana with it. Each character is introduced with a page number on the video so you can easily find the practice sheet.

A practice sheet for each character is designed to provide less help as you progress in writing a character. Hence, each practice sheet includes five different practice patterns.

Although some of you may have already been exposed to Roma-ji (Roman characters), it is essential that you do not rely on Roma-ji for the pronunciation and actual writing of Japanese.

For Katakana characters, refer to the second volume of this series.

Organization

This workbook consists of three parts. Part one is designated for 46 basic Hiragana; part two is for 25 Hiragana with the consonants [g, z, d, j, b, and p]; and part three is for 36 Hiragana with the semi-vowel [y]. The characters presented in part two and part three are all deviations from some of the characters practiced in part one.

Each part contains a chart of Hiragana for pronunciation practice, notes on usage and pronunciation, stroke practice sheets, and recognition and dictation exercises. Answers for the exercises are provided at the end of this workbook. The video demonstrates correct pronunciation and stroke order and presents the exercises. Basic patterns for each part are as follows.

On the Video

At the beginning of each part, you will see a chart of the Hiragana characters which are to be practiced there. Practice the pronunciation of the characters with the chart and the video. Then you will see instructions on usage and pronunciation.

After studying usage and pronunciation of some special characters, you will see a pattern like this:

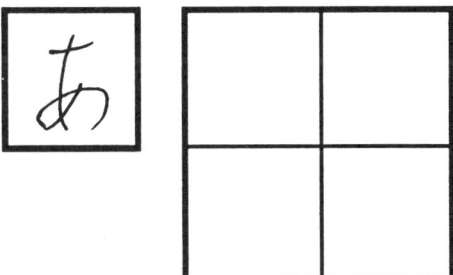

In the small square, a character is written. The stroke order of this character will be demonstrated in the larger square which has quadrants to indicate the appropriate positions of each stroke. The correct pronunciation of the character will be demonstrated at the same time. A page number is also announced on the video so that you can find the practice sheet easily. As a result of the demonstration, you will see the product on the screen like the one below:

 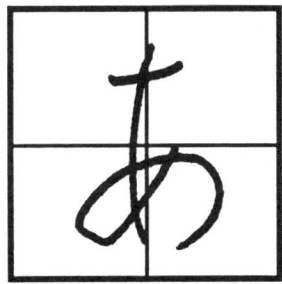

Some of the characters look alike, and are confusing in their appearance. Observe the stroke order very carefully. Then try it in the workbook. Practice the pronunciation as you practice the stroke(s).

(REMEMBER: stroke order is very important!)

How to Use This Workbook

In the Workbook

In the workbook, you will see the following sections. Again, this workbook is designed for use with the accompanying videotape, which demonstrates the stroke order and the pronunciation of Hiragana. Please get the maximum benefit from both materials. Use the sense of sight and oral, aural, and motor skills to develop independence in Japanese writing.

Pronunciation Practice:

At the beginning of each part, you will see a chart of the Hiragana characters which are to be practiced. Practice pronunciation with the videotape before you start practicing the stroke(s).

Notes on Usage and Pronunciation:

This section lists some characters which require special instructions. On the practice sheets, some characters are marked with a note number. When those characters appear, check the "Note" section, and make sure you read those special instructions. Although the closest pronunciations of the example words are given in [ ], refer to the videotape for the correct pronunciation of the words.

Stroke Practice Sheet:

You will see five practice patterns for each character. For best results, it is highly recommended to replay the videotape from time to time to assure that you are practicing correctly. These five sections are organized in a progress sequence to develop your independence in writing Japanese. The more you progress, the less support is provided.

I. Tracing

In the far left square, the example of a character is presented. Dotted lines are provided in the following squares. Trace the dotted lines that help in writing the character. Also, pronounce the character each time you trace it in order to establish a firm association between the pronunciation and the character. The pattern used for this practice looks like this:

 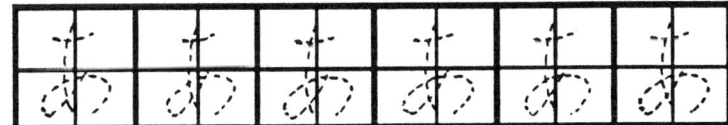

II. Writing with quadrants

Continue practicing the stroke(s) of the same character. However, this time, there are no dotted lines. Make sure your writing is correct. Refer to the example and the video from time to time. Again, pronounce the character each time you write it in order to establish a firm association between the correct pronunciation and the character. The pattern for this practice looks like this:

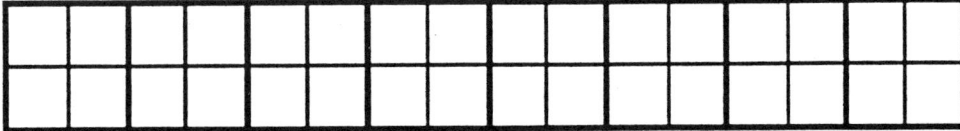

III. Writing with and without quadrants

Continue practicing the stroke(s) of the same character with no dotted lines. However, this time, the squares are alternately supplied with quadrants. Try not to rely on visible quadrants. Make sure that your stroke(s) are correct by referring to the example and to the video. Pronounce the character each time you write it in order to establish a firm association between the correct pronunciation and the character. The pattern for this practice looks like this:

IV. Writing without quadrants

In the far left square, the example of the same character is presented. The squares for this practice do not have quadrants. Continue practicing the stroke(s) of the same character. Pronounce the character each time you write it in order to establish a firm association between the correct pronunciation and character. The pattern used for this practice looks like this:

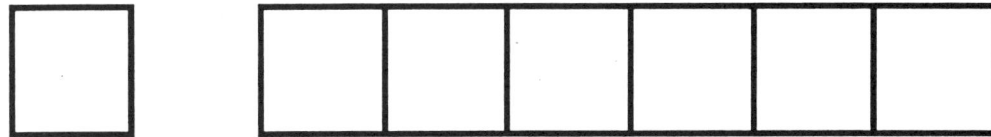

V. Free-standing

Continue practicing the stroke(s) of the same character without the squares. As you can see, the size of the character is small, which is more appropriate for actual writing. Pronounce the character each time you write it for establishing a firm association between the correct pronunciation and the character. The pattern used for this practice looks like this:

L__I__I__I__I__I__I__I__I__I__I__I__I__I__I__J

Recognition and Dictation Exercise:

In addition to the stroke and pronunciation practices, there are recognition and dictation exercises at the end of each part. In the recognition exercises you will be asked to pronounce some characters after seeing them or to recognize visually some charcters after hearing them. In the dictation exercises, you will be asked to write some vocabulary words. The answers, except for the first type of recognition exercise, are supplied at the end of this workbook. Check the answers and practice writing those words. If possible, it is highly recommended that you check them with a native speaker of Japanese.

PART I

46 BASIC HIRAGANA CHARACTERS

Directions:
1. Practice pronunciation of 46 basic Hiragana characters with the chart and the videotape.

2. Read the notes and practice pronunciation with the videotape.

3. Observe the stroke order of 46 basic Hiragana characters on the videotape and try it on the practice sheets.

4. Do the exercises.

Chart of 46 Basic Hiragana Characters

Practice pronunciation with the videotape before you start practicing the stroke(s). Be aware that each character is a syllable and pronounced with equal length. The note numbers are indicated to the right of the characters which require special attention. The characters in this chart may be slightly different from the ones you are to practice, but both are perfectly correct.

1. あ　い　う -1　え　お
2. か　き　く　け　こ
3. さ　し　す　せ　そ
4. た -2　ち　つ -3　て -2　と -2
5. な　に　ぬ　ね　の
6. は -4　ひ　ふ -5　へ -6　ほ
7. ま　み　む　め　も
8. や　　　ゆ　　　よ
9. ら -7　り -7　る -7　れ -7　ろ -7
10. わ　　　　　　　　を -8
11. ん -9

Notes on Usage and Pronunciation

The following list explains Hiragana characters which require special notes. Since they involve problems concerning pronunciation, it is essential that you read this section and study with the videotape which accompanies this workbook.

On the practice sheets, some characters are marked with a note number. When the note number appears, come back to this section and make sure that you know the proper usage of the character.

Vocabulary words presented in this list are followed by [ ] and ( ). The closest pronunciations, not Roma-ji, of the words are indicated by [ ], and the English equivalents for the words are indicated by ( ). Again, for the correct pronunciation, refer to the videotape as often as possible.

1. う   Although "う" is normally pronounced like [*u*], it should be pronounced very softly when it is used to indicate a long vowel. Usually it occurs in the middle or at the end of a word. When "う" is used at the beginning of a word, it has a full sound. Practice and compare the pronunciation of the following words with the video tape.

Full sound			Soft sound		
うみ	[*umi*]	(an ocean)	とうきょう	[*tokyo*]	(Tokyo)
うさぎ	[*usagi*]	(a rabbit)	がっこう	[*ga ko*]	(a school)
うち	[*uchi*]	(a house)	きょう	[*kyo*]	(today)

2. た、て、and と
   Although they start with the consonant sound [*t*], it is a very weak [*t*] sound. Try to relax the tongue and pronounce them. Pay attention to the pronunciation demonstration on the video.

3. つ   First, pronounce the English word "cats," then rememner the position of the tip of the tongue. Pronounce this [*ts*] sound a couple of times and then add the vowel to form a syllable. As a result it should sound like [*tsu*]; however, it is still only one syllable long. Pay attention to the pronunciation demonstrated on the video.

   Although "つ" is normally pronounced like [*tsu*], a small "つ" is used to indicate that the consonant immediately following it receives double length. Practice and compare the following pairs with the video tape.

   1. もと   [*moto*] (an origin)   もっと   [*mo to*] (more)
   2. よか   [*yoka*] (leisure time)   よっか   [*yo ka*] (4th day of a month)
   3. がか   [*gaka*] (an artistic painter) がっか   [*ga ka*] (an academic subject)

4. は   Although "は" is normally pronounced like [*ha*], it should be pronounced like "わ"[*wa*] when "は" is used as a subject indicator. <u>Never</u> write "わ" to indicate the subject.

5. ふ   Since English [*f*] sound does not exist in Japanese, do not pronounce ふ like [*fu*]. Pronounce ふ like [*hu*]; however, for the correct pronunciation, refer to the videotape. Those who have already studied Japanese using Roma-ji should check the pronunciation because all the textbooks employing Roma-ji use the symbols "fu" for ふ sound.

Part I: 46 Basic Hiragana Characters

6. **へ**   Although "へ" is nomally pronounced like [*heh*], it should be pronounced like "え" [*eh*] when it is used to indicate direction or destination. <u>Never</u> write "え" or pronounce [*eh*] to indicate direction or destination.

7. **らりるれ and ろ**

   Do not pronounce らりるれろ with [*l*] or [*r*] sounds. Practice らりるれろ sounds with the videotape very carefully. These sounds are flapping sounds, pronounced with the tip of the tongue first touching briefly against the upper tooth ridge and then flicked downward. Those who have already studied Japanese using Roma-ji should check the pronunciation because all the textbooks employing Roma-ji use the symbol "r" for these sounds.
   *The Spanish soft [*r*] sound is very close to the Japanese [*r*] sound.

8. **を**   Although "お"[*o*] and "を"[*o*] are pronounced the same, "を" is used to indicate a direct object. <u>Never</u> write "お" to indicate the direct object.

9. **ん**   This character is pronounced rather ambiguously depending upon the consonant immediately following it.

   1. Before the consonant sounds [*b, m,* or *p*], it is pronounced like an English [*m*] as in (man).

      1. ぜんぶ   [*zembu*]   (whole)
      2. かんむり   [*kam muli*]   (a crown)
      3. しんぱい   [*shimpeye*]   (anxiety)

   2. Before the consonant sounds [*d, n, t,* or *z*], it is pronounced like an English [*n*] as in (nail).

      1. こんど   [*kondo*]   (this time)
      2. おんな   [*on na*]   (woman)
      3. かんたん   [*kantan*]   (simple)
      4. ぎんざ   [*ginza*]   (Ginza)

   3. Before the consonant sounds [*k,* or *g*] and at the end of a word, it is pronounced like an English [*ng*] as in (ring).

      1. げんかい   [*gengkeye*]   (a limit)
      2. おんがく   [*ongaku*]   (music)

Part I: 46 Basic Hiragana Characters

I. Trace

II. Writing with quadrants

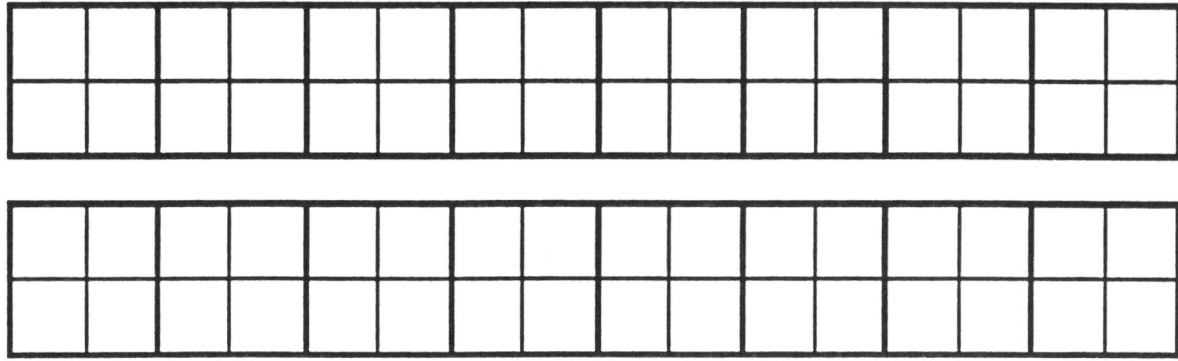

III. Writing with and without quadrants

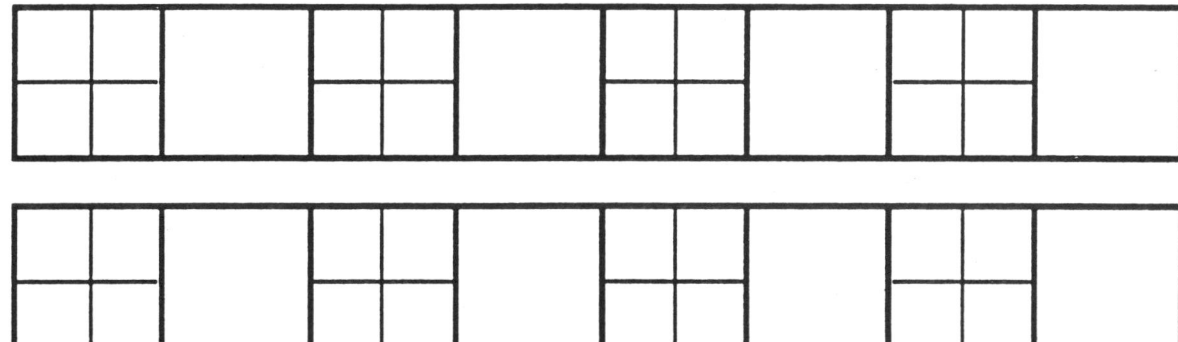

IV. Writing without quadrants

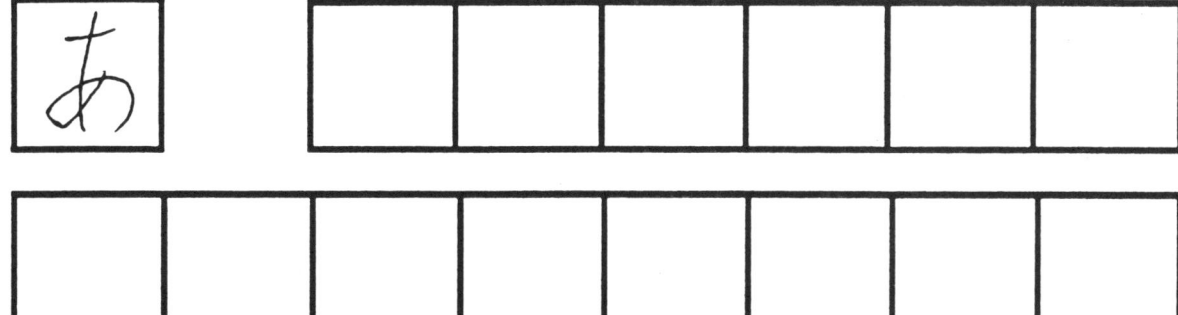

V. Free-standing

あ　あ

Part I: 46 Basic Hiragana Characters

I. Trace

II. Writing with quadrants

III. Writing with and without quadrants

IV. Writing without quadrants

V. Free-standing

Part I: 46 Basic Hiragana Characters

I. Trace

Note-1

II. Writing with quadrants

III. Writing with and without quadrants

IV. Writing without quadrants

V. Free-standing

Part I: 46 Basic Hiragana Characters

I. Trace

II. Writing with quadrants

III. Writing with and without quadrants

IV. Writing without quadrants

V. Free-standing

Part I: 46 Basic Hiragana Characters

I. Trace

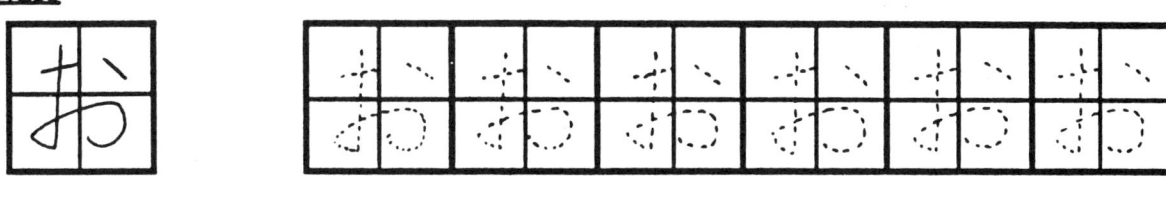

II. Writing with quadrants

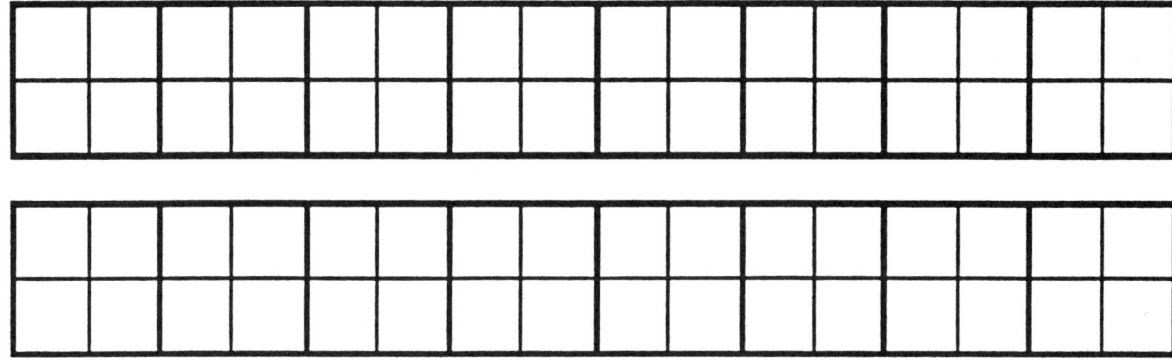

III. Writing with and without quadrants

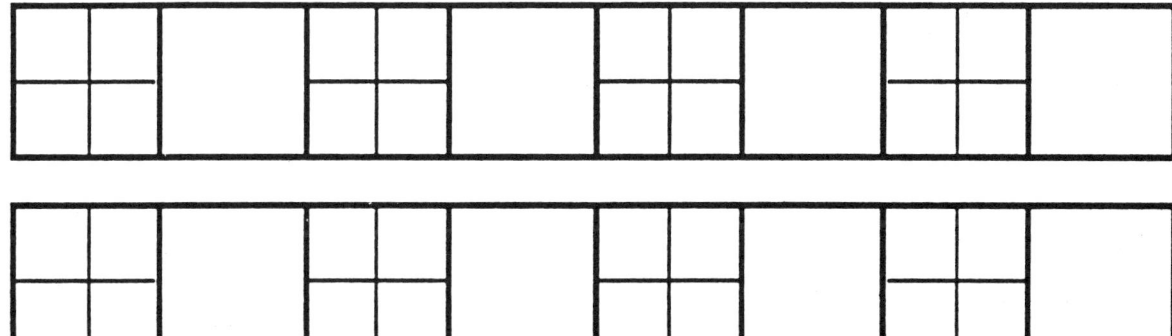

IV. Writing without quadrants

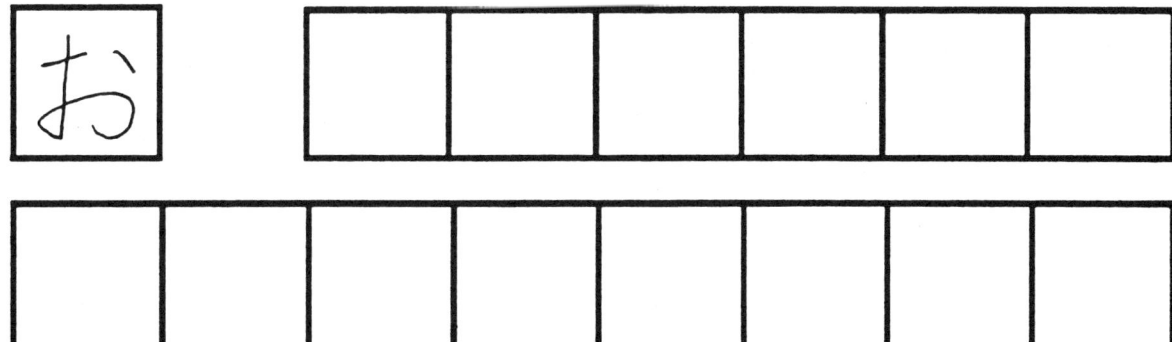

V. Free-standing

Part I: 46 Basic Hiragana Characters

I. Trace

II. Writing with quadrants

III. Writing with and without quadrants

IV. Writing without quadrants

V. Free-standing

Part I: 46 Basic Hiragana Characters

I. Trace

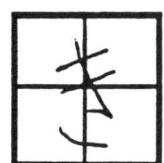

II. Writing with quadrants

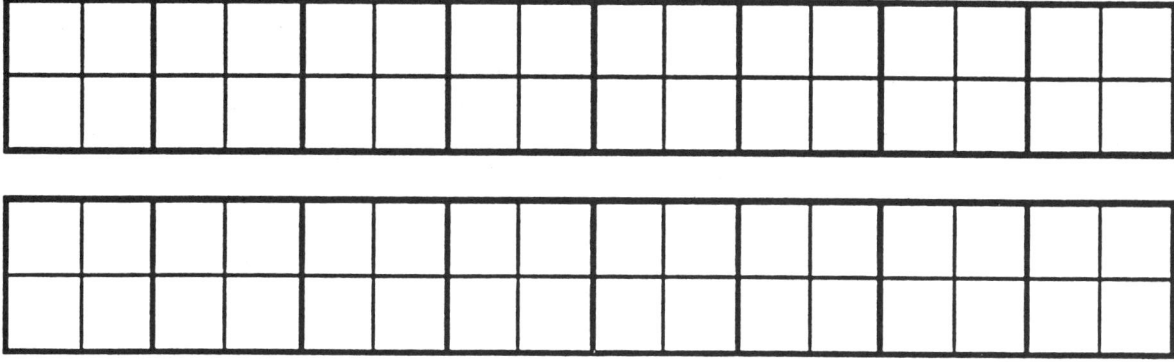

III. Writing with and without quadrants

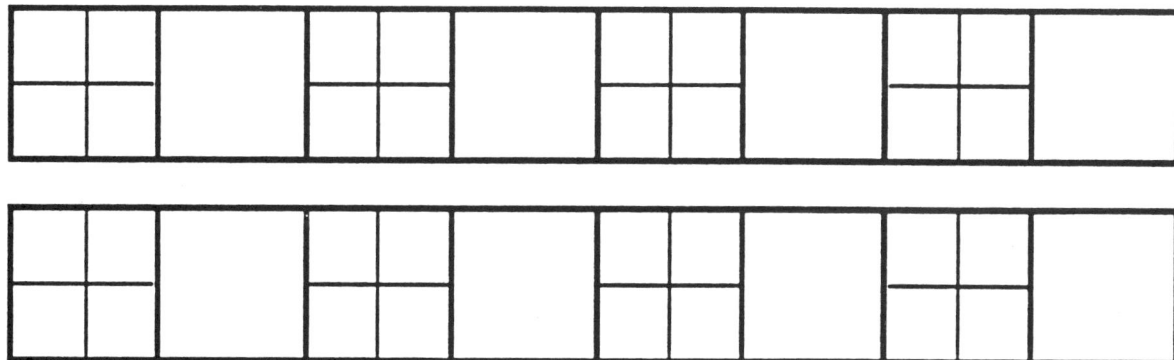

IV. Writing without quadrants

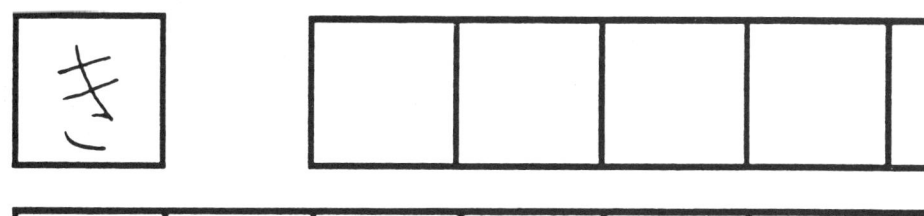

V. Free-standing

Part I: 46 Basic Hiragana Characters

I. Trace

II. Writing with quadrants

III. Writing with and without quadrants

IV. Writing without quadrants

V. Free-standing

Part I: 46 Basic Hiragana Characters

I. Trace

II. Writing with quadrants

III. Writing with and without quadrants

IV. Writing without quadrants

V. Free-standing

Part I: 46 Basic Hiragana Characters

I. Trace

II. Writing with quadrants

III. Writing with and without quadrants

IV. Writing without quadrants

V. Free-standing

Part I: 46 Basic Hiragana Characters

I. Trace

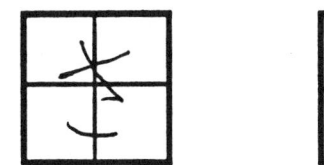 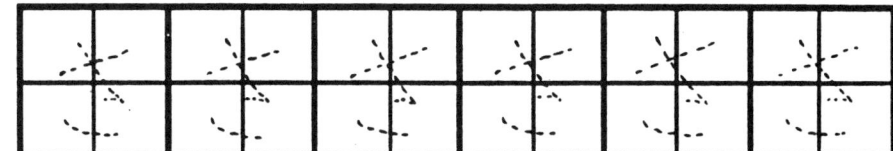

II. Writing with quadrants

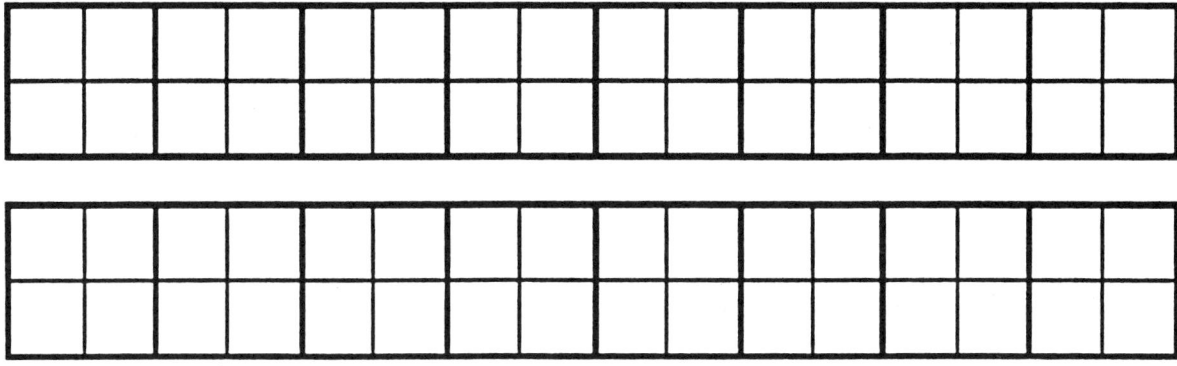

III. Writing with and without quadrants

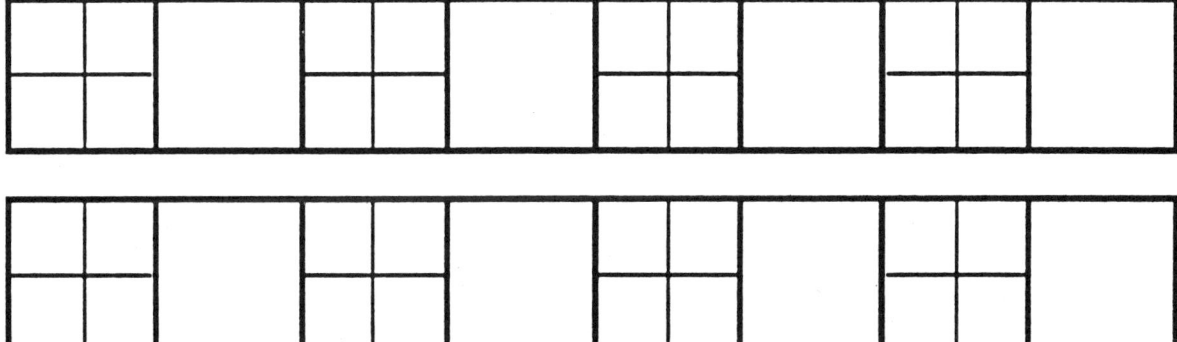

IV. Writing without quadrants

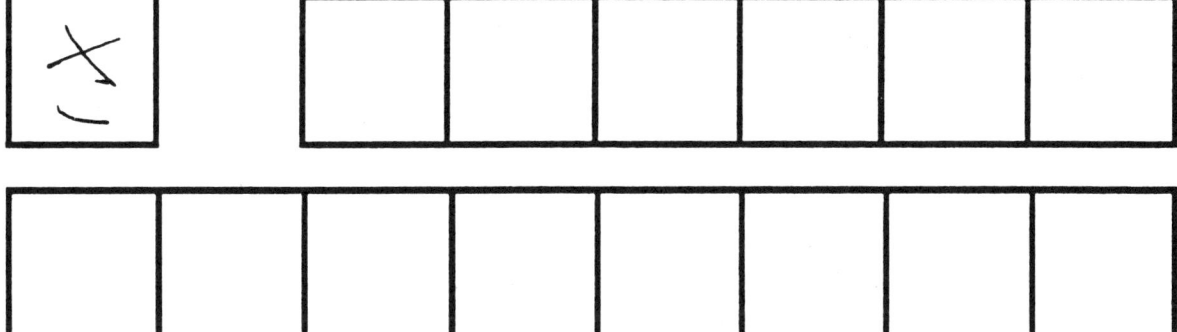

V. Free-standing

Part I: 46 Basic Hiragana Characters

I. Trace

II. Writing with quadrants

III. Writing with and without quadrants

IV. Writing without quadrants

V. Free-standing

Part I: 46 Basic Hiragana Characters

I. Trace

II. Writing with quadrants

III. Writing with and without quadrants

IV. Writing without quadrants

V. Free-standing

Part I: 46 Basic Hiragana Characters

I. Trace

II. Writing with quadrants

III. Writing with and without quadrants

IV. Writing without quadrants

V. Free-standing

Part I: 46 Basic Hiragana Characters

I. Trace

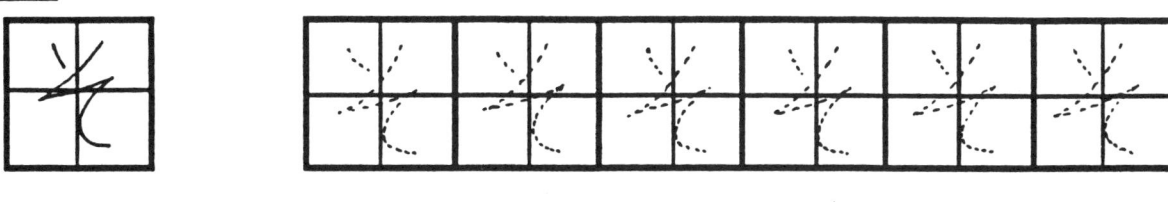

II. Writing with quadrants

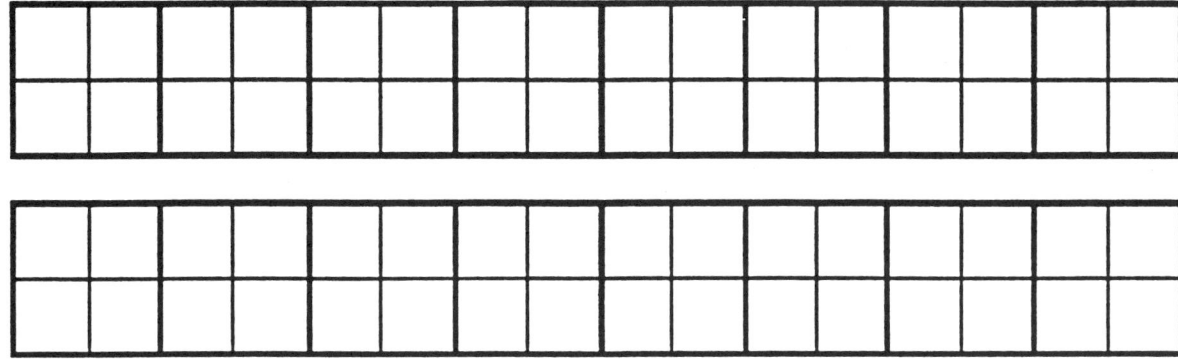

III. Writing with and without quadrants

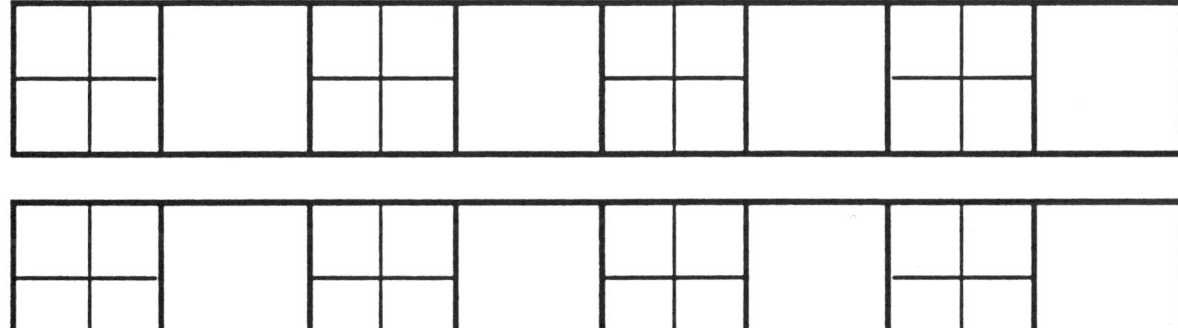

IV. Writing without quadrants

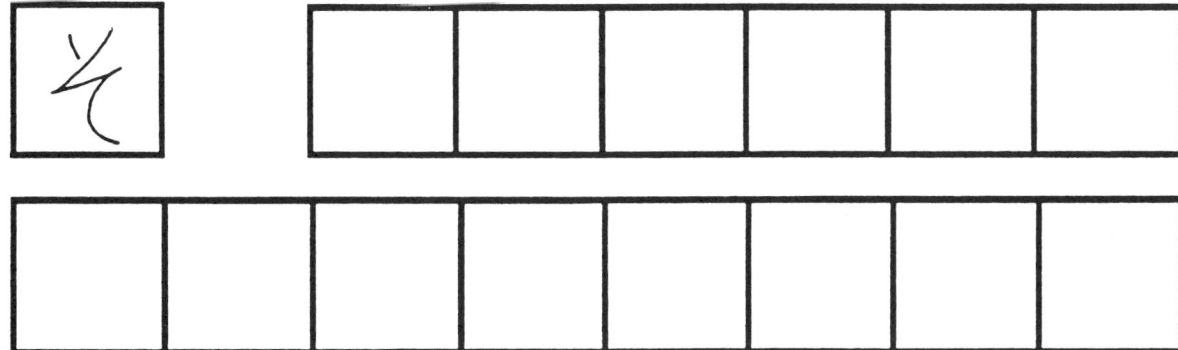

V. Free-standing

そ　そ

Part I: 46 Basic Hiragana Characters

I. Trace

Note-2

II. Writing with quadrants

III. Writing with and without quadrants

IV. Writing without quadrants

V. Free-standing

Part I: 46 Basic Hiragana Characters

I. Trace

II. Writing with quadrants

III. Writing with and without quadrants

IV. Writing without quadrants

V. Free-standing

Part I: 46 Basic Hiragana Characters

I. Trace

Note-3

II. Writing with quadrants

III. Writing with and without quadrants

IV. Writing without quadrants

V. Free-standing

Part I: 46 Basic Hiragana Characters

I. Trace

Note-2

II. Writing with quadrants

III. Writing with and without quadrants

IV. Writing without quadrants

V. Free-standing

Part I: 46 Basic Hiragana Characters

I. Trace

Note-2

II. Writing with quadrants

III. Writing with and without quadrants

IV. Writing without quadrants

V. Free-standing

Part I: 46 Basic Hiragana Characters

I. Trace

II. Writing with quadrants

III. Writing with and without quadrants

IV. Writing without quadrants

V. Free-standing

Part I: 46 Basic Hiragana Characters

I. Trace

II. Writing with quadrants

III. Writing with and without quadrants

IV. Writing without quadrants

V. Free-standing

Part I: 46 Basic Hiragana Characters

I. Trace

II. Writing with quadrants

III. Writing with and without quadrants

IV. Writing without quadrants

V. Free-standing

Part I: 46 Basic Hiragana Characters

I. Trace

II. Writing with quadrants

III. Writing with and without quadrants

IV. Writing without quadrants

V. Free-standing

Part I: 46 Basic Hiragana Characters

I. Trace

II. Writing with quadrants

III. Writing with and without quadrants

IV. Writing without quadrants

V. Free-standing

Part I: 46 Basic Hiragana Characters

I. Trace

Note-4

II. Writing with quadrants

III. Writing with and without quadrants

IV. Writing without quadrants

V. Free-standing

Part I: 46 Basic Hiragana Characters

I. Trace

II. Writing with quadrants

III. Writing with and without quadrants

IV. Writing without quadrants

V. Free-standing

Part I: 46 Basic Hiragana Characters

I. Trace

Note-5

II. Writing with quadrants

III. Writing with and without quadrants

IV. Writing without quadrants

V. Free-standing

Part I: 46 Basic Hiragana Characters

I. Trace

Note-6

II. Writing with quadrants

III. Writing with and without quadrants

IV. Writing without quadrants

V. Free-standing

Part I: 46 Basic Hiragana Characters

I. Trace

ほ

II. Writing with quadrants

III. Writing with and without quadrants

IV. Writing without quadrants

ほ

V. Free-standing

ほ ほ

Part I: 46 Basic Hiragana Characters

I. Trace

II. Writing with quadrants

III. Writing with and without quadrants

IV. Writing without quadrants

V. Free-standing

Part I: 46 Basic Hiragana Characters

I. Trace

II. Writing with quadrants

III. Writing with and without quadrants

IV. Writing without quadrants

V. Free-standing

Part I: 46 Basic Hiragana Characters

I. Trace

II. Writing with quadrants

III. Writing with and without quadrants

IV. Writing without quadrants

V. Free-standing

Part I: 46 Basic Hiragana Characters

I. Trace

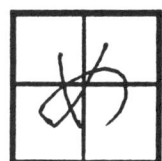 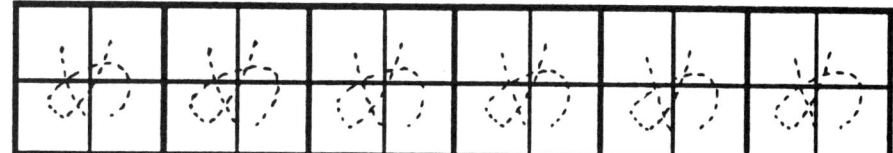

II. Writing with quadrants

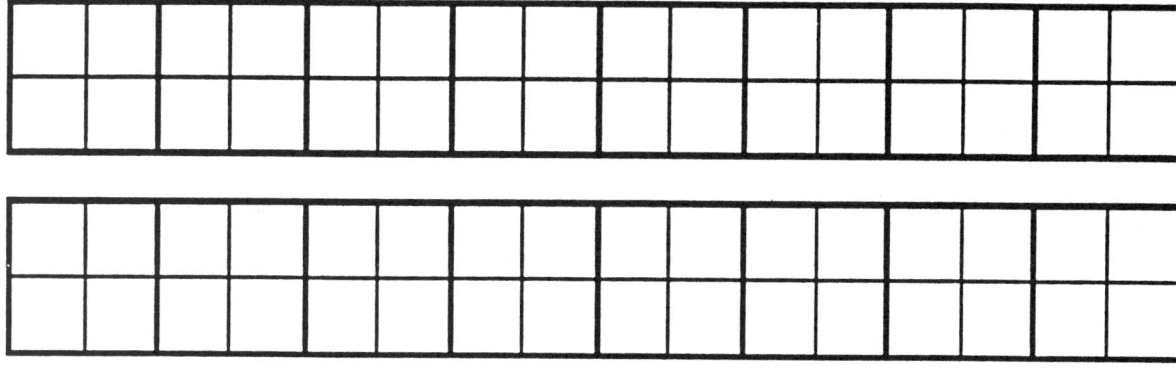

III. Writing with and without quadrants

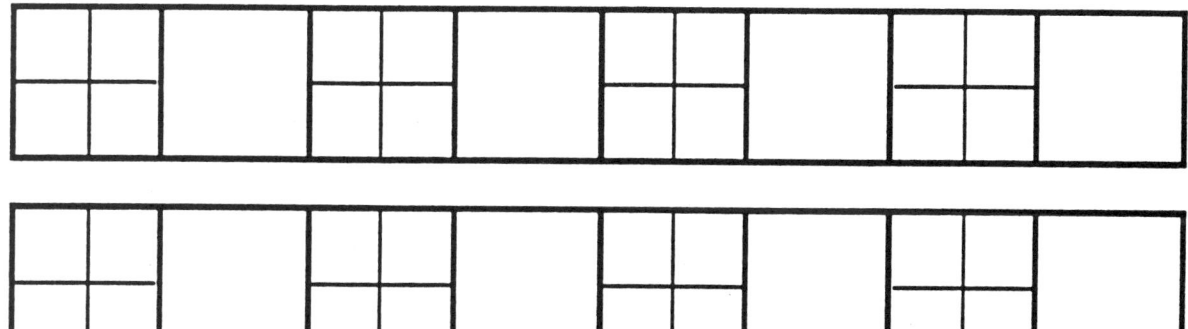

IV. Writing without quadrants

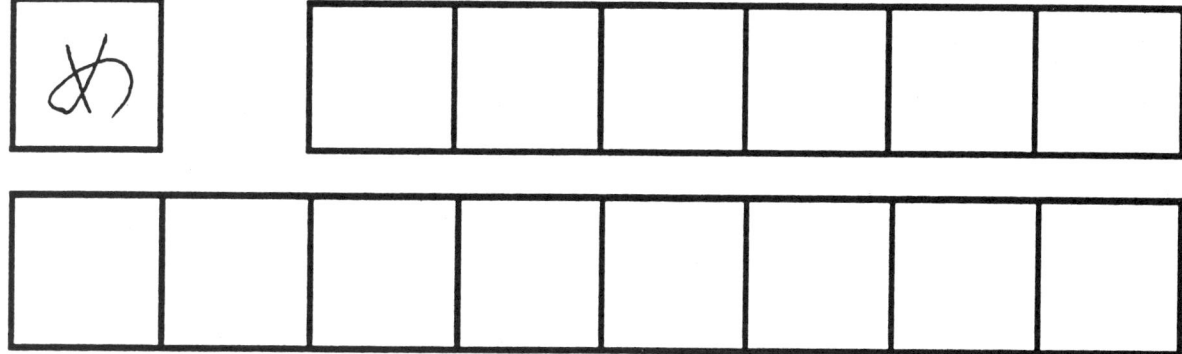

V. Free-standing

Part I: 46 Basic Hiragana Characters

I. Trace

II. Writing with quadrants

III. Writing with and without quadrants

IV. Writing without quadrants

V. Free-standing

Part I: 46 Basic Hiragana Characters

I. Trace

II. Writing with quadrants

III. Writing with and without quadrants

IV. Writing without quadrants

V. Free-standing

Part I: 46 Basic Hiragana Characters

I. Trace

II. Writing with quadrants

III. Writing with and without quadrants

IV. Writing without quadrants

V. Free-standing

Part I: 46 Basic Hiragana Characters

I. Trace

II. Writing with quadrants

III. Writing with and without quadrants

IV. Writing without quadrants

V. Free-standing

Part I: 46 Basic Hiragana Characters

I. Trace

Note-7

II. Writing with quadrants

III. Writing with and without quadrants

IV. Writing without quadrants

V. Free-standing

Part I: 46 Basic Hiragana Characters 47

I. Trace

Note-7

II. Writing with quadrants

III. Writing with and without quadrants

IV. Writing without quadrants

V. Free-standing

Part I: 46 Basic Hiragana Characters

I. Trace

Note-7

II. Writing with quadrants

III. Writing with and without quadrants

IV. Writing without quadrants

V. Free-standing

Part I: 46 Basic Hiragana Characters

I. Trace

Note-7

II. Writing with quadrants

III. Writing with and without quadrants

IV. Writing without quadrants

V. Free-standing

Part I: 46 Basic Hiragana Characters

I. Trace

Note-7

II. Writing with quadrants

III. Writing with and without quadrants

IV. Writing without quadrants

V. Free-standing

Part I: 46 Basic Hiragana Characters

I. Trace

II. Writing with quadrants

III. Writing with and without quadrants

IV. Writing without quadrants

V. Free-standing

Part I: 46 Basic Hiragana Characters

I. Trace

Note-8

II. Writing with quadrants

III. Writing with and without quadrants

IV. Writing without quadrants

V. Free-standing

Part I: 46 Basic Hiragana Characters

I. Trace

Note-9

II. Writing with quadrants

III. Writing with and without quadrants

IV. Writing without quadrants

V. Free-standing

Part I: 46 Basic Hiragana Characters

Exercises

Correct answers are presented in APPENDIX A. The characters used in the following exercises may be slightly different from the ones you practiced; however, both are perfectly correct.

Exercise A:
On the video, 10 characters are shown. Pronounce each character and check if you have pronounced it correctly. Answers will be given immediately following the question on the video. Hence, answers for this exercise are not given in APPENDIX A.

Exercise B:
On the video, 15 Hiragana characters are pronounced. Find the characters in the chart below. Answer by indicating the number-letter combination which corresponds with the correct character.

Example: If す is pronounced, answer 7-D because す is found at the cross point between 7 and D in the chart below.

	A	B	C	D	E
1.	さ	と	の	は	る
2.	き	よ	な	か	ち
3.	い	み	け	た	や
4.	ん	く	え	し	ろ
5.	ま	つ	ふ	ね	へ
6.	ゆ	こ	う	ら	わ
7.	む	れ	め	す	そ
8.	あ	せ	も	お	に
9.	て	ほ	ぬ	り	ひ

Answer here:

1. _____   6. _____   11. _____
2. _____   7. _____   12. _____
3. _____   8. _____   13. _____
4. _____   9. _____   14. _____
5. _____   10. _____   15. _____

Continue this exercise with your instructor and fellow students or a Japanese friend.

Part I: 46 Basic Hiragana Characters

Exercise C:

On the video, a Japanese word is pronounced. Find the word in the list of words below. Choose the word and answer with the letter assigned to the left of the word.

1.   a. はち   b. たな   c. はな   d. わた

2.   a. ねむい   b. くもり   c. めくる   d. ぬるい

3.   a. ほし   b. うし   c. はし   d. けし

4.   a. たき   b. あさ   c. かさ   d. ゆき

5.   a. こい   b. ここ   c. もり   d. かに

Continue this exercise with your instructor and fellow students or a Japanese friend.

Exercise D:

On the video, a Japanese word is pronounced. Write the word in Hiragana below. Each space is for one character.

1. ____ ____

2. ____ ____

3. ____ ____ ____ ____

4. ____ ____ ____

5. ____ ____

6. ____ ____ ____

7. ____ ____

8. ____ ____ ____

9. ____ ____

10. ____ ____ ____

11. ____ ____

12. ____ ____

13. ____ ____ ____

14. ____ ____

15. ____ ____

PART II

25 HIRAGANA CHARACTERS

WITH CONSONANTS:
[g, z, d, j, b, p]

Directions:
1. Practice pronunciation of the 25 Hiragana characters with the chart and the videotape.

2. Read the notes and practice pronunciation with the videotape.

3. Observe the stroke order of the 25 Hiragana characters on the videotape and try it on the practice sheets.

4. Do the exercises.

Chart of 25 Hiragana Characters
With Consonants: [g, z, d, j, b, p]

The "ひらがな" to be practiced in this part are presented below. These are basically the same as some of the "ひらがな" practiced in part I, but with some additional markers. Two dots added to the upper right corner of the character signify that the consonants *k*, *s*, *t*, and *h* have become *g*, *z*, *d* or *j*, and *b*, respectively. The circle added to the upper right corner of the character signifies that the consonant *b* has become *p*. Recall, for example, か [*ka*] from part one and compare with が [*ga*], the first letter in this chart. Note numbers are indicated to the right of the characters.

Now, practice pronunciation with the video tape.

1. が　ぎ　ぐ　げ　ご

2. ざ　じ -1　ず -2　ぜ　ぞ

3. だ　ぢ -1　づ -2　で　ど

4. ば　び　ぶ　べ　ぼ

5. ぱ　ぴ　ぷ　ぺ　ぽ

Notes on Usage and Pronunciation

1. じ and ぢ — Both are pronounced the same: [*ji*]. However, they are not interchangeable in writing. Misuse creates wrong spelling and, sometimes, wrong meaning.

   Although じ is usually used, when you find this sound within a word, except at the beginning, look it up in the dictionary. ぢ is used where the sound [*chi*] is changed into [*ji*] in a compound word.

   (There are only four words starting with ぢ .)

2. ず and づ — Both are pronounced the same: [*zu*]. However, they are not interchangeable in writing. Misuse creates wrong spelling and, sometimes, wrong meaning.

   Although ず is usually used, when you find this sound within a word, except at the beginning, look it up in the dictionary. づ is used where the sound [*tsu*] is changed into [*zu*] in a compound word.

   (There is no word starting with づ .)

Part II: 25 Hiragana Characters with Consonants: [g, z, d, j, b, p]

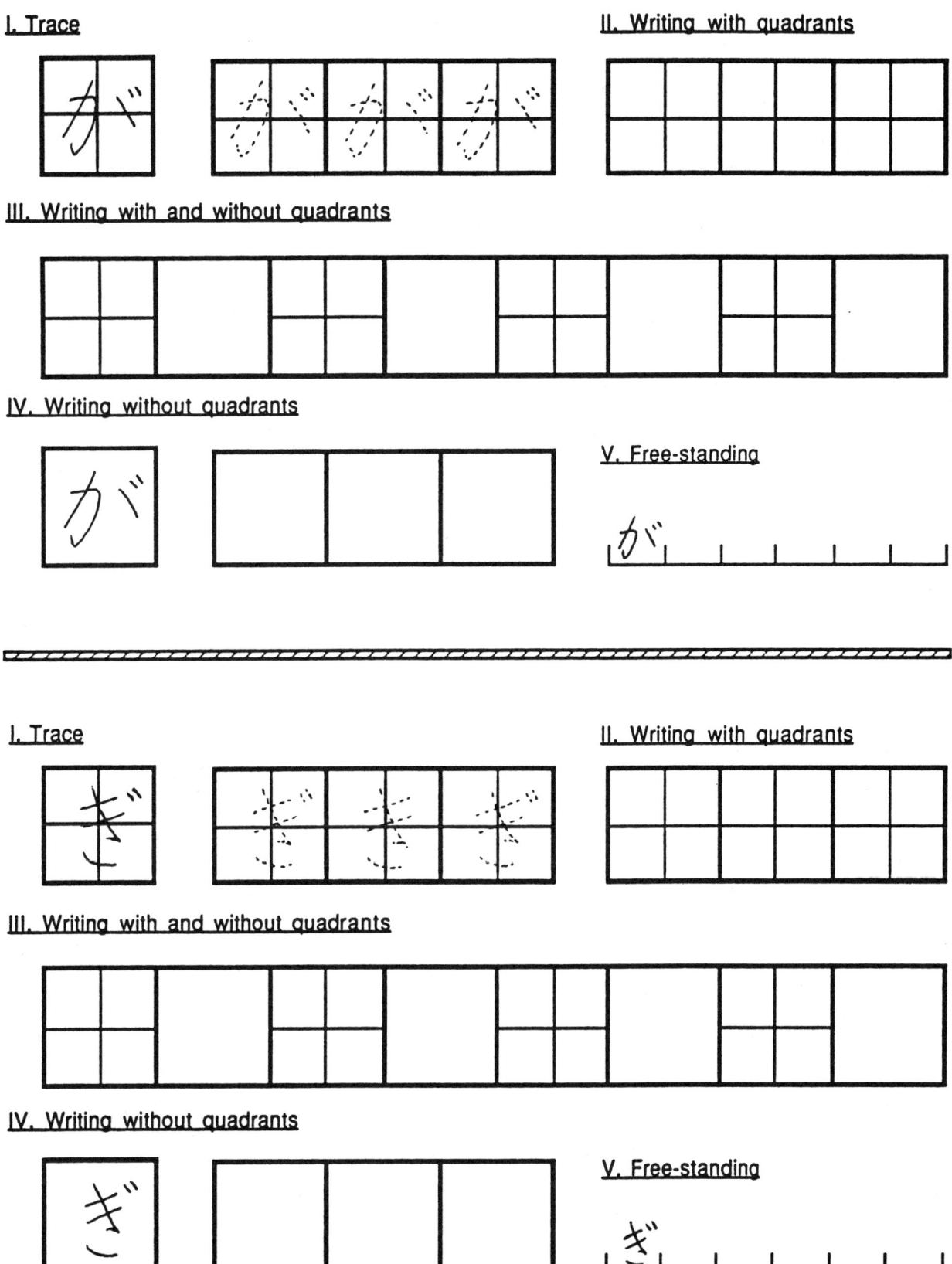

Part II: 25 Hiragana Characters with Consonants: [g, z, d, j, b, p]

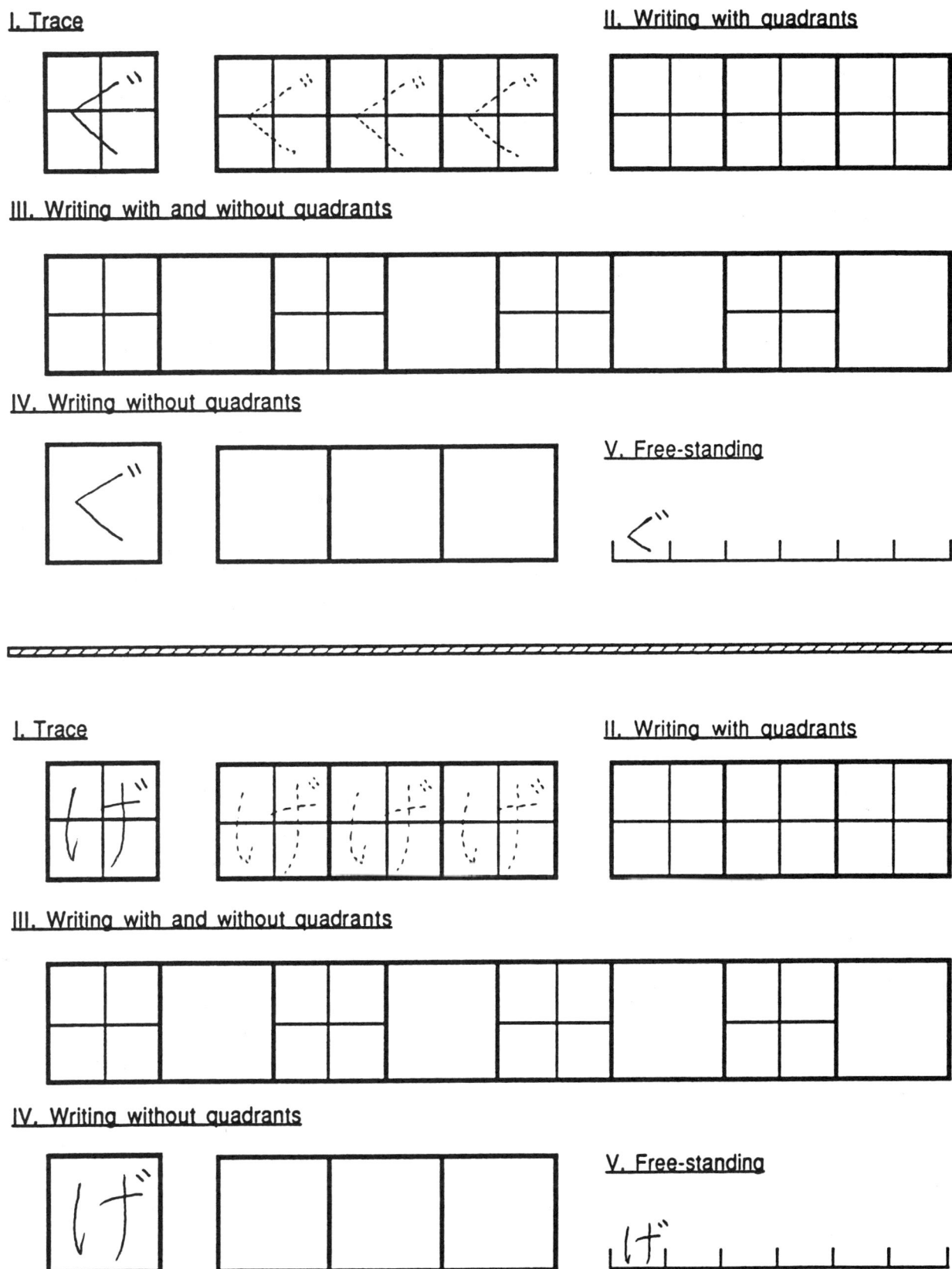

Part II: 25 Hiragana Characters with Consonants: [g, z, d, j, b, p]

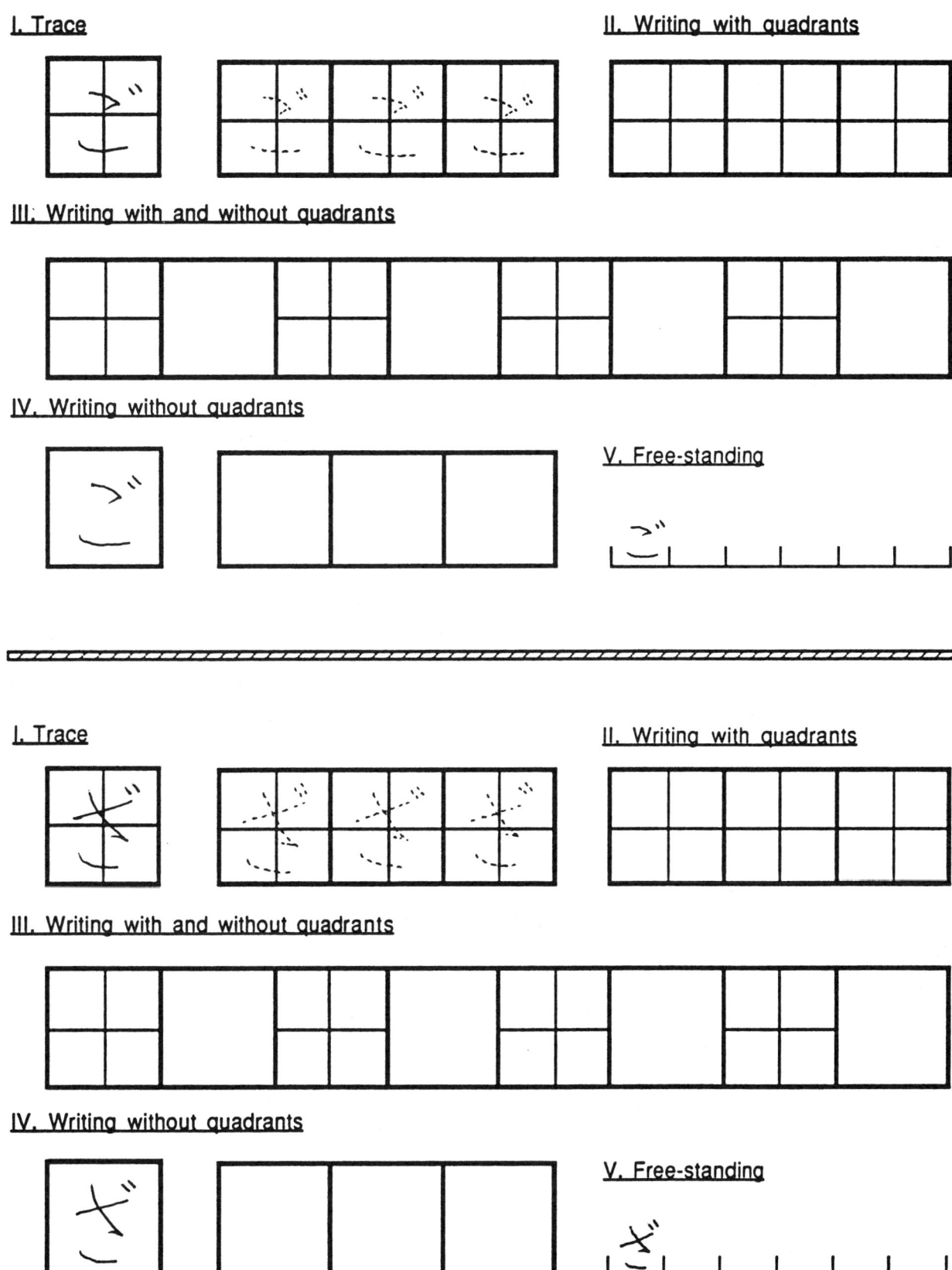

Part II: 25 Hiragana Characters with Consonants: [g, z, d, j, b, p]

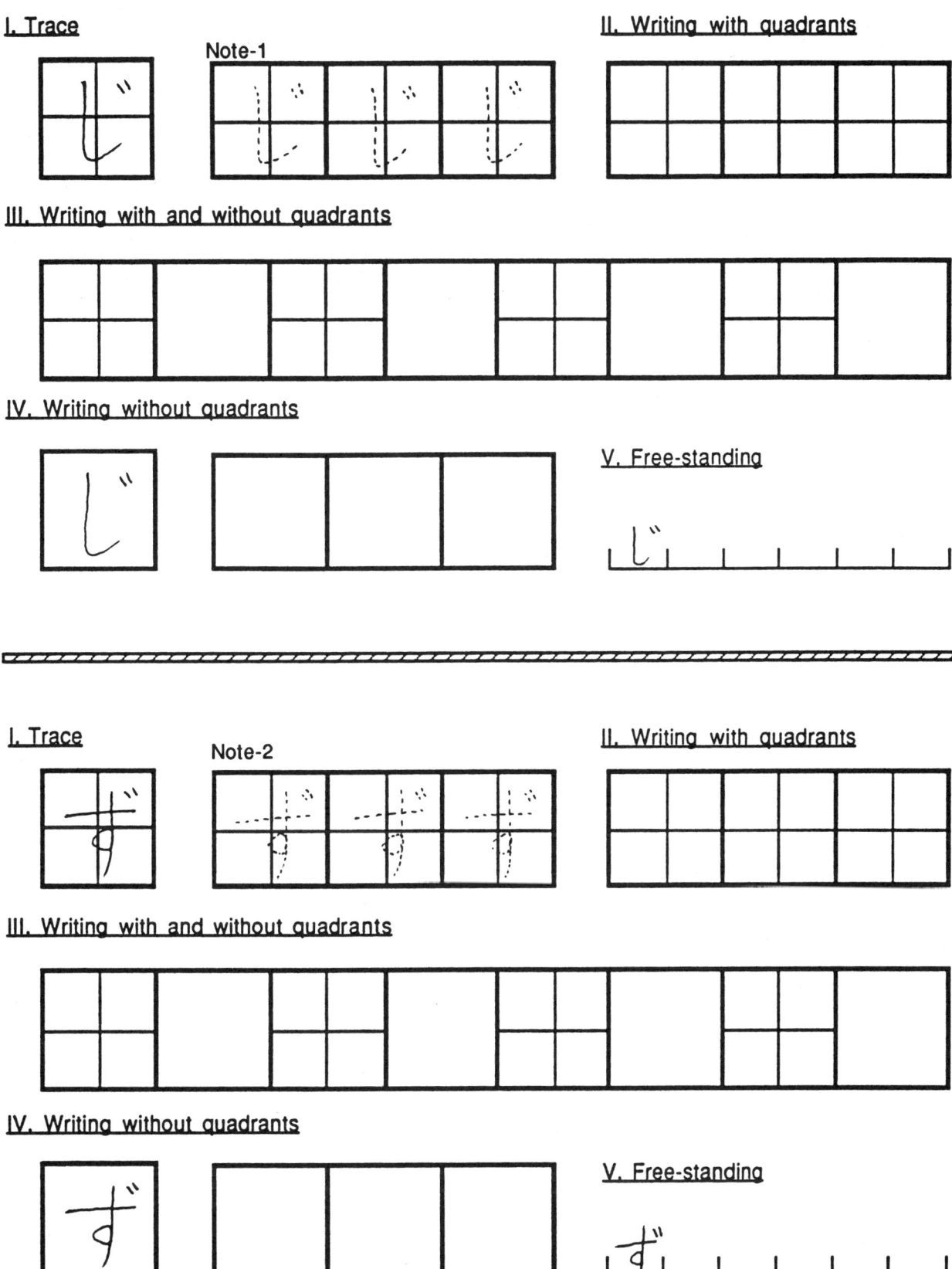

Part II: 25 Hiragana Characters with Consonants: [g, z, d, j, b, p]

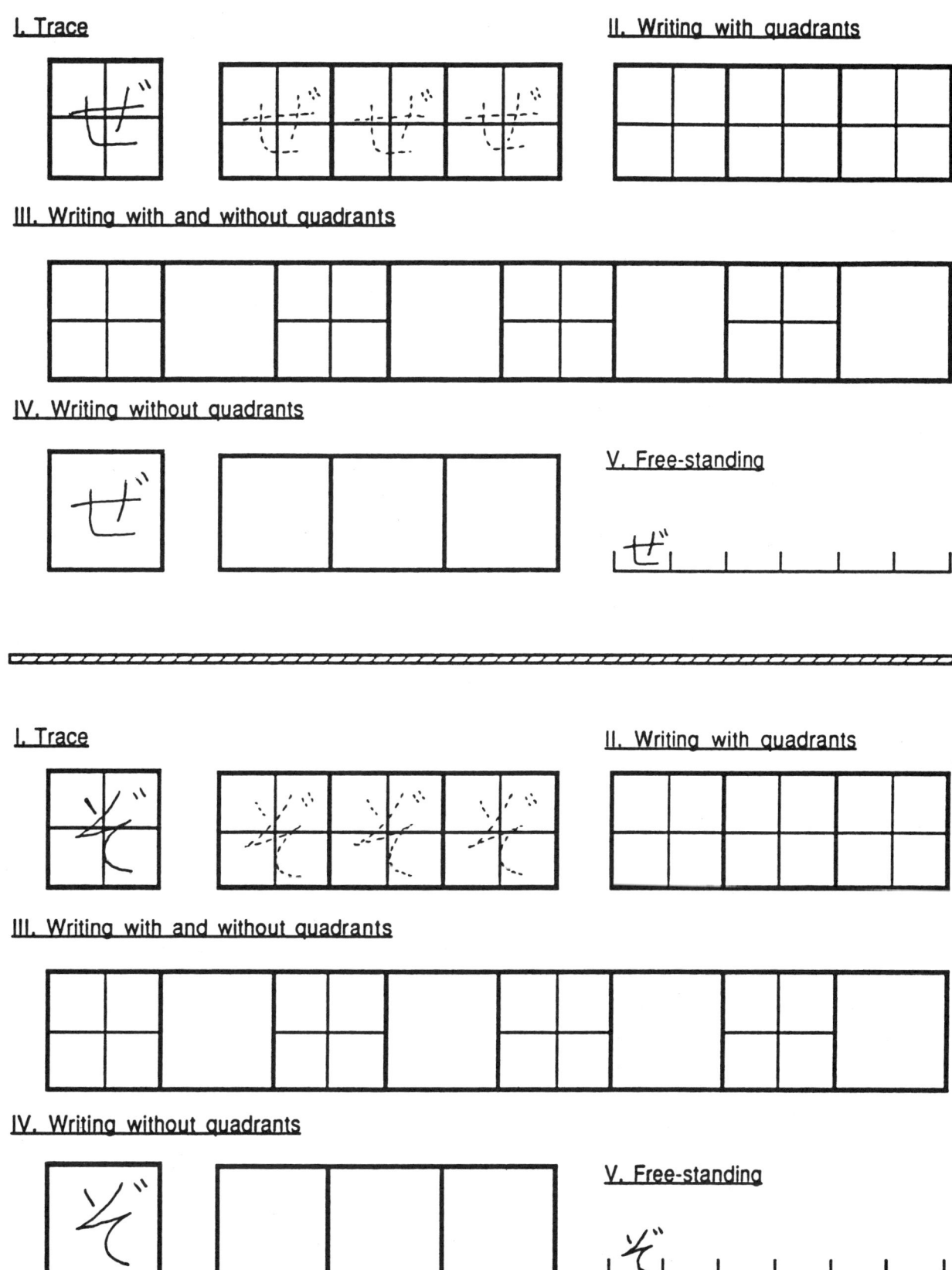

Part II: 25 Hiragana Characters with Consonants: [g, z, d, j, b, p]

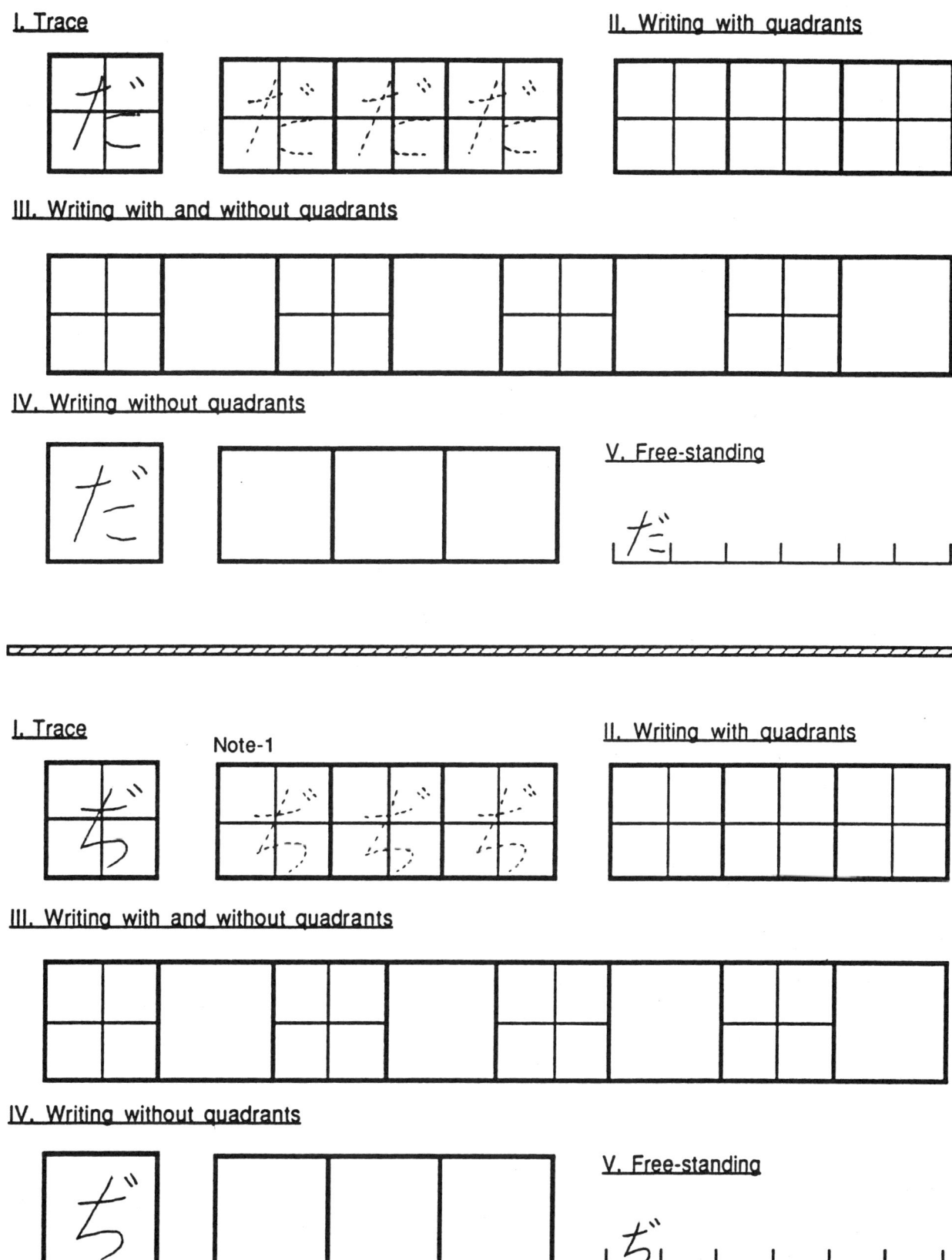

Part II: 25 Hiragana Characters with Consonants: [g, z, d, j, b, p]

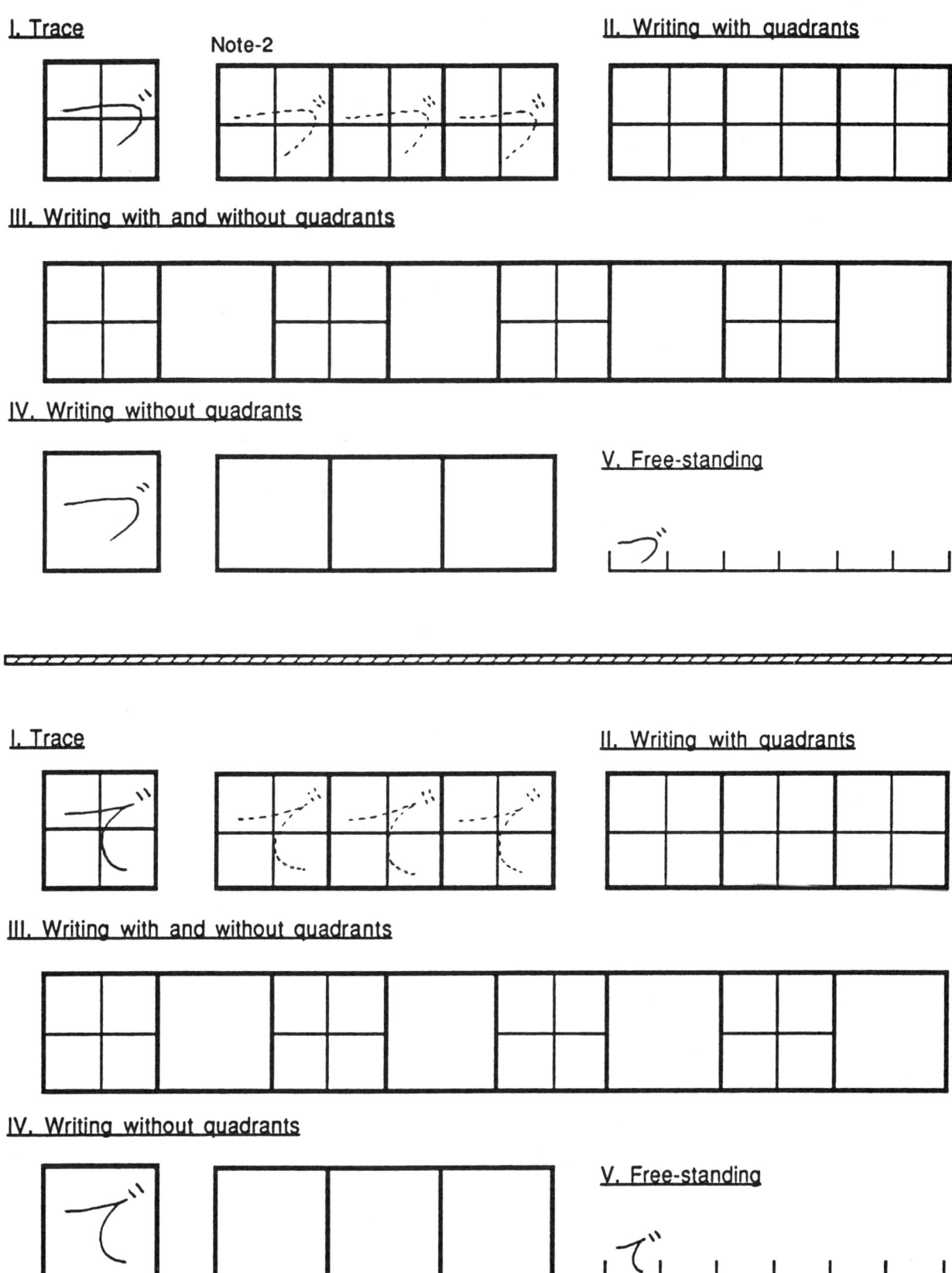

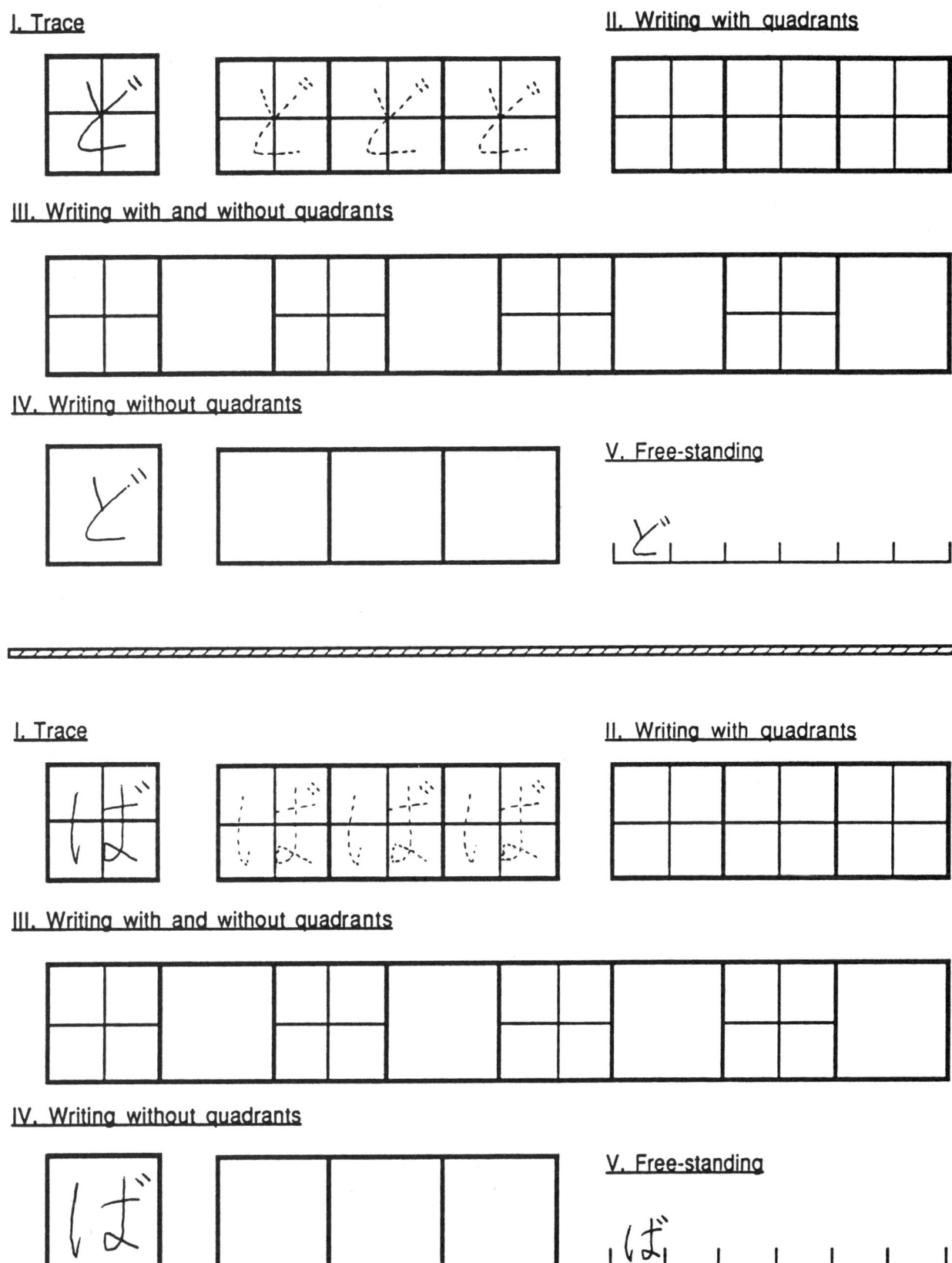

Part II: 25 Hiragana Characters with Consonants: [g, z, d, j, b, p]

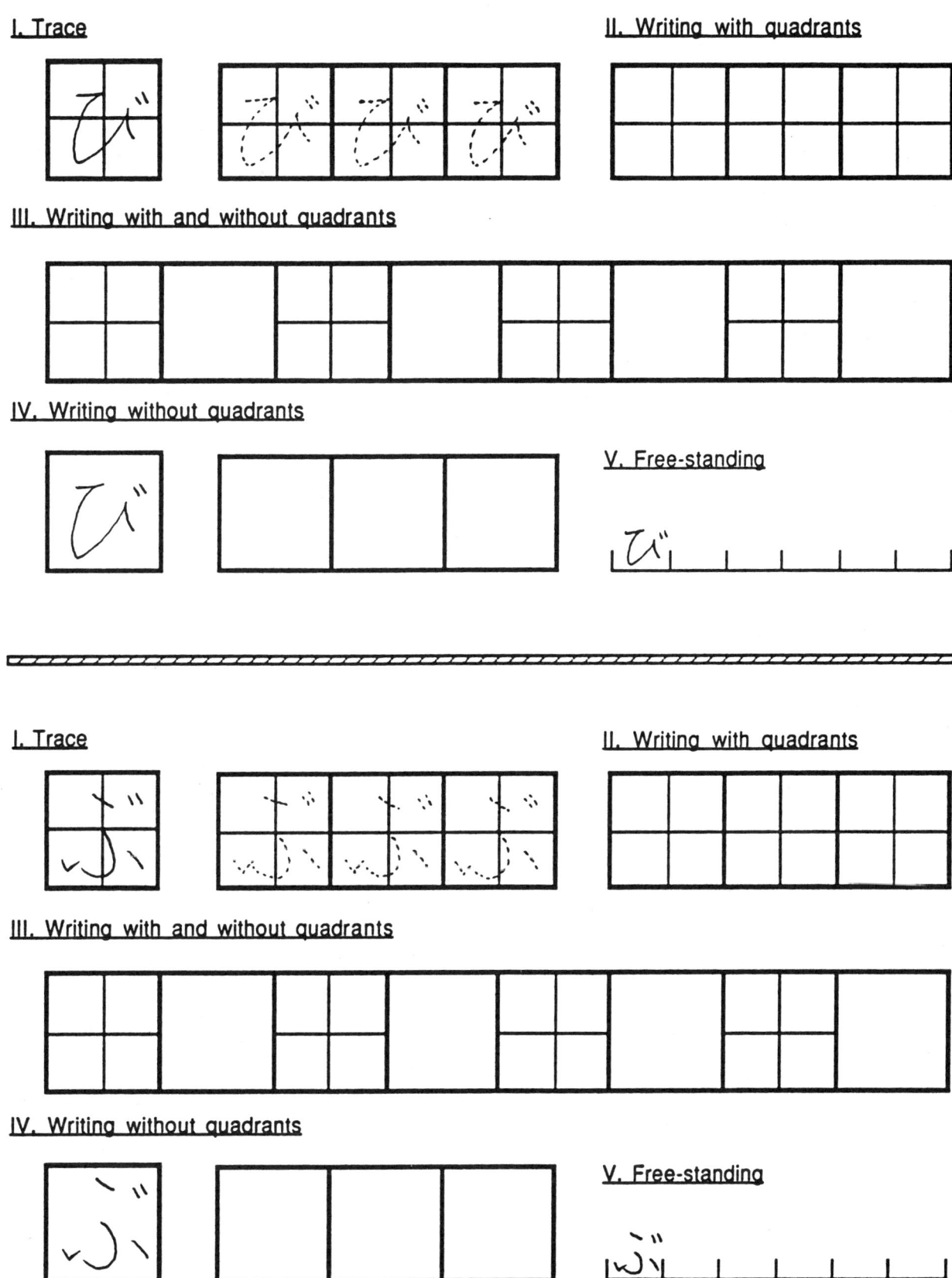

Part II: 25 Hiragana Characters with Consonants: [g, z, d, j, b, p]

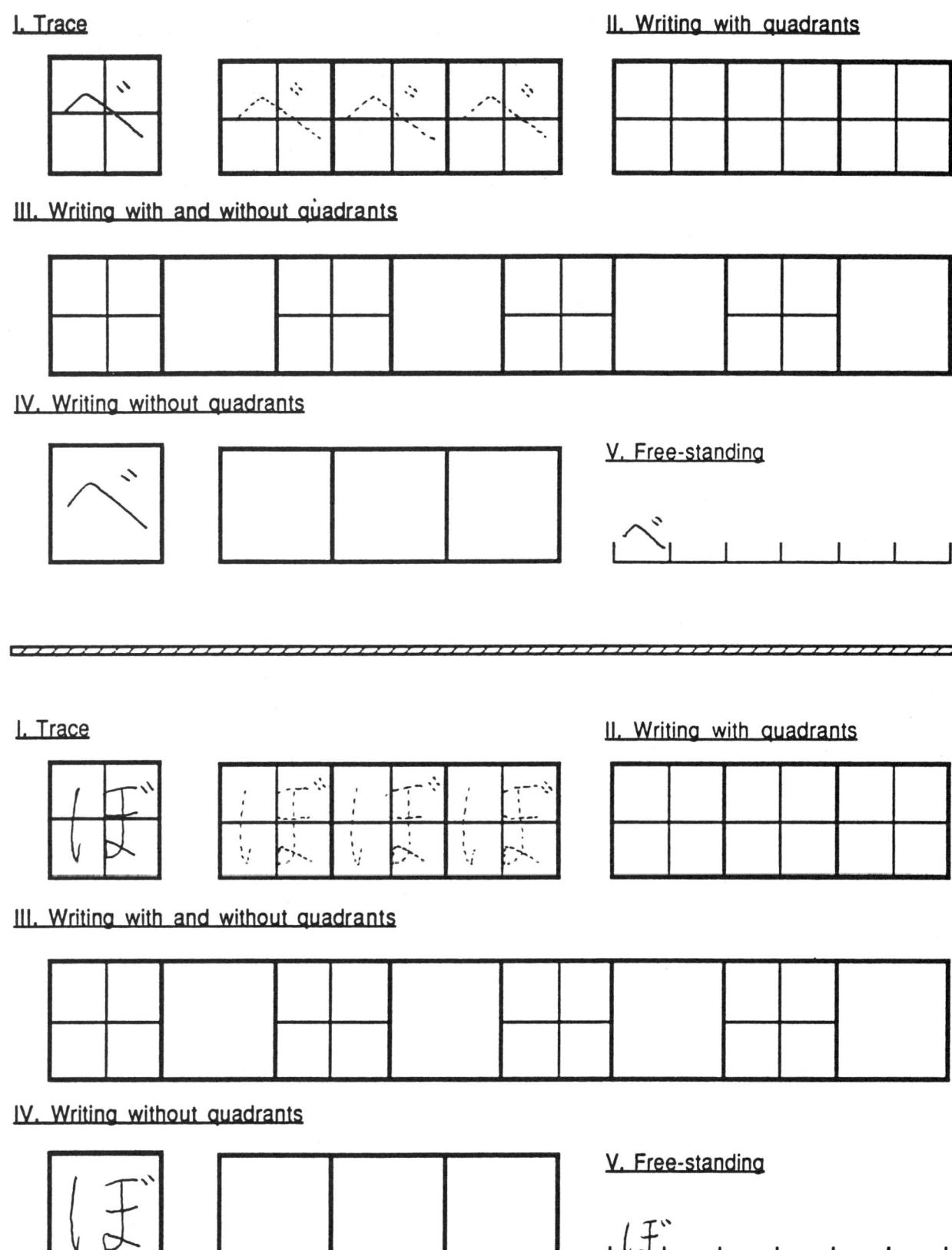

Part II: 25 Hiragana Characters with Consonants: [g, z, d, j, b, p]

I. Trace

II. Writing with quadrants

III. Writing with and without quadrants

IV. Writing without quadrants

V. Free-standing

ぱ

I. Trace

II. Writing with quadrants

III. Writing with and without quadrants

IV. Writing without quadrants

V. Free-standing

ぴ

Part II: 25 Hiragana Characters with Consonants: [g, z, d, j, b, p]   69

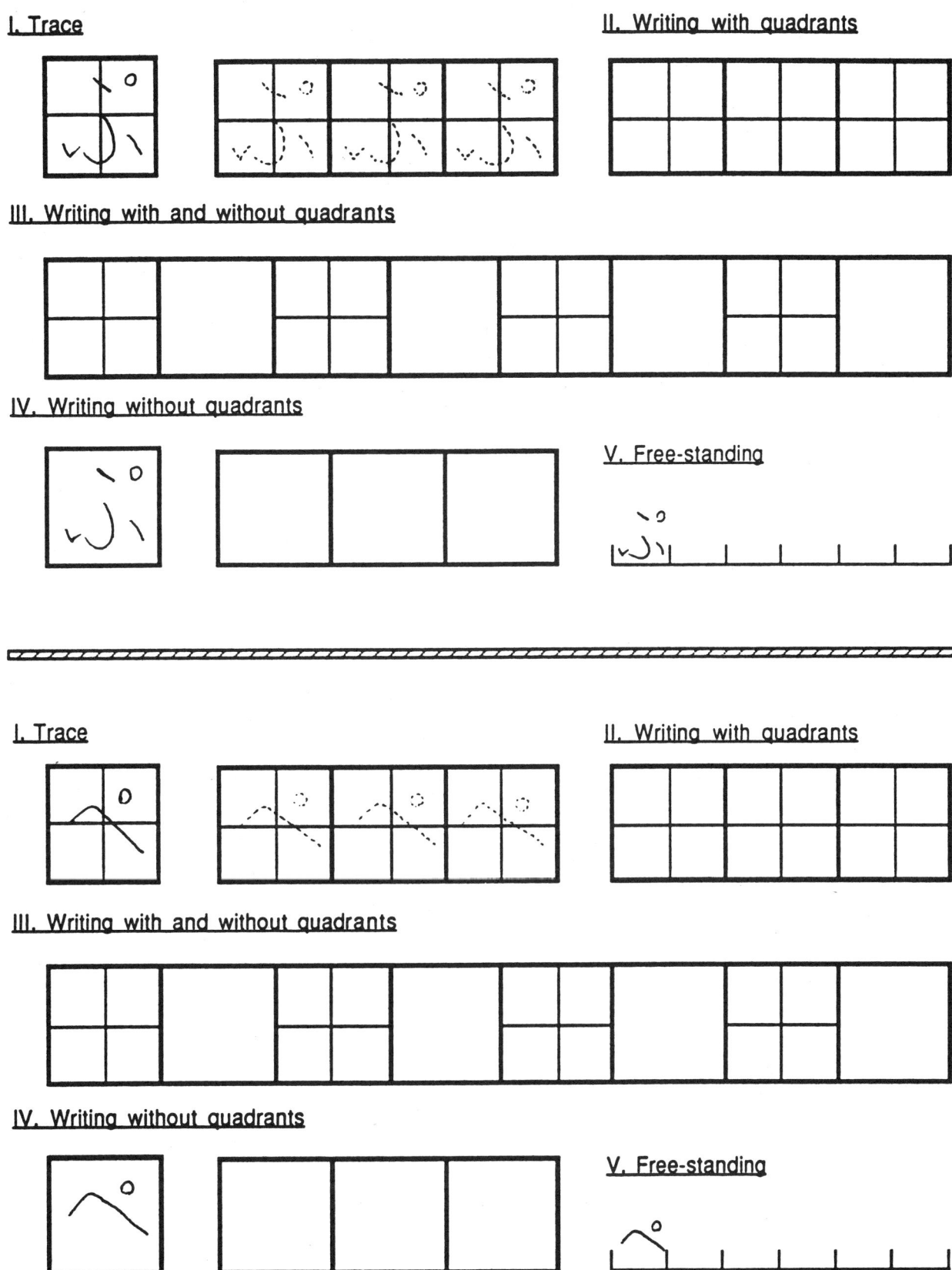

Part II: 25 Hiragana Characters with Consonants: [g, z, d, j, b, p]

I. Trace

II. Writing with quadrants

III. Writing with and without quadrants

IV. Writing without quadrants

V. Free-standing

I. Trace

II. Writing with quadrants

III. Writing with and without quadrants

IV. Writing without quadrants

V. Free-standing

Part II: 25 Hiragana Characters with Consonants: [g, z, d, j, b, p]

Exercises

Correct answers are presented in APPENDIX A. The characters used in the following exercises may be slightly different from the ones you practiced; however, both are perfectly correct.

Exercise A:
On the video, 10 characters are shown. Pronounce each character and check if you have pronounced it correctly. Answers will be given immediately following the question on the video. Hence, answers for this exercise are not given in APPENDIX A.

Exercise B:
On the video, 15 Hiragana characters are pronounced. Find the characters in the chart below. Answer by indicating the number-letter combination which corresponds with the correct character.

Example: If が is pronounced, answer 3-B because が is found at the cross point between 3 and B in the chart below.

	A	B	C	D	E
1.	ぎ	だ	ぜ	ば	ご
2.	び	ぢ	べ	げ	ぞ
3.	ぱ	が	ざ	ぼ	ぷ
4.	じ	ぴ	づ	ぶ	ど
5.	で	ず	ぺ	ぐ	ぽ

Answer here:

1. _____   6. _____   11. _____
2. _____   7. _____   12. _____
3. _____   8. _____   13. _____
4. _____   9. _____   14. _____
5. _____   10. _____   15. _____

Continue this exercise with your instructor and fellow students or a Japanese friend.

Exercise C:

On the video, a Japanese word is pronounced. Find the word in the list of words below. Choose the word and answer with the letter assigned to the left of the word.

1. a. ざっし b. ぶっし c. じっし d. ばっし

2. a. かんじ b. でんぶ c. じぶん d. こんぶ

3. a. ぎん b. びん c. がん d. だん

4. a. はっぷん b. えんぴつ c. しゅっぱん d. うっかり

5. a. ちがい b. ごかい c. にがい d. にかい

Continue this exercise with your instructor and fellow students or a Japanese friend.

Exercise D:

On the video, a Japanese word is pronounced. Write the word in Hiragana below. Each space is for one character.

1. ____ ____ ____ ____
2. ____ ____ ____ ____
3. ____ ____ ____
4. ____ ____
5. ____ ____ ____
6. ____ ____ ____
7. ____ ____ ____
8. ____ ____ ____ ____
9. ____ ____ ____
10. ____ ____ ____
11. ____ ____ ____
12. ____ ____ ____ ____
13. ____ ____
14. ____ ____ ____
15. ____ ____ ____

PART III

36 HIRAGANA CHARACTERS

WITH
SEMI-VOWEL: [y]

Directions:
1. Practice pronunciation of the 36 Hiragana characters with the chart and the videotape.

2. Read the notes and practice pronunciation with the videotape.

3. Observe the stroke order of the 36 Hiragana characters on the videotape and try it on the practice sheets.

4. Do the exercises.

Chart of 36 Hiragana Characters
with
Semi-Vowel: [y]

The "ひらがな" to be practiced in this part are presented below. These are basically the same as some of the "ひらがな" practiced in part I and II, but with small や, ゆ, and よ. Again, each character is one syllable long. Hence, duration of sound is exactly the same as that of other "ひらがな". Therefore, do not pronounce きや, for example, like [ki-ya] forming two syllables. Pronounce it like [kya] as one syllable. Note numbers are indicated to the right of the characters.

Now, <u>listen to the video very carefully</u> and practice pronunciation.

1. きゃ   きゅ   きょ
2. ぎゃ   ぎゅ   ぎょ
3. しゃ   しゅ   しょ
4. じゃ -2 じゅ -2 じょ -2
5. ちゃ   ちゅ   ちょ
6. ぢゃ -2 ぢゅ -2 ぢょ -2
7. にゃ   にゅ   にょ
8. ひゃ   ひゅ   ひょ
9. びゃ   びゅ   びょ
10. ぴゃ   ぴゅ   ぴょ
11. みゃ   みゅ   みょ
12. りゃ -3 りゅ -3 りょ -3

Part III: 36 Hiragana Characters with Semi-Vowel: [y]

Notes on Usage and Pronunciation

1. When written vertically

    Although you will practice horizontal writing, Japanese may be written vertically. When written vertically, the characters to be practiced in this part look like the examples presented below. The numbers correspond to the the line numbers in the chart.

    Notice the position of small や, ゆ, and よ in relation to the bigger part. When documents are written vertically, you need to read from right to left and each line from top to bottom. In other words, in the examples below, first read line 1 from top to bottom, then read line 2 from top to bottom and so on.

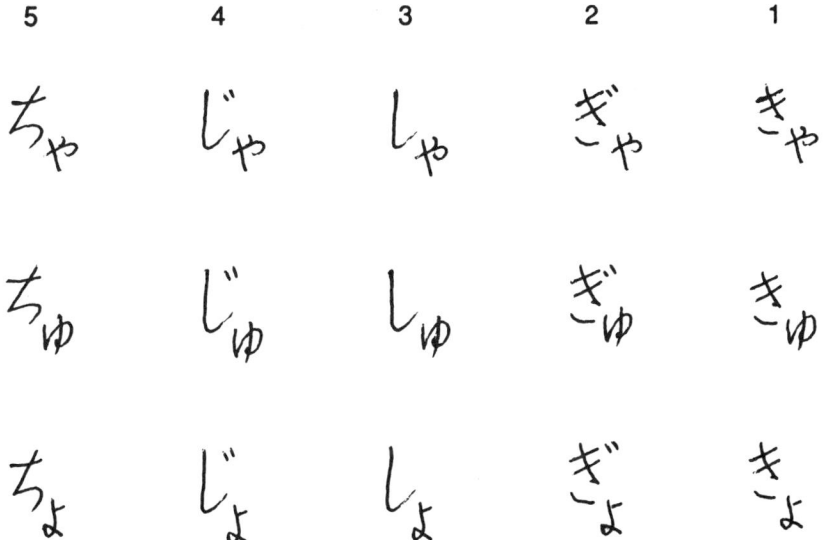

2. じゃ、じゅ、じょ and
   ぢゃ、ぢゅ、ぢょ

    The difference between じゃ、じゅ、じょ and ぢゃ、ぢゅ、ぢょ is not a matter of pronunciation but one of usage, as it was between じ and ぢ. Although ぢゃ, ぢゅ, and ぢょ are still used in some compound words as in the example below, they are practically unused in Japanese today. Hence, it is always safe to use じゃ、じゅ、and じょ.
    Since ぢゃ, ぢゅ, and ぢょ are practically unused, the practice sheets for these characters are not included in this workbook.

    Example:
    ちゃわん(tea cup) = まっちゃぢゃわん (a cup used for tea ceremony)

3. りゃ, りゅ and りょ

    As it was pointed out earlier, the English [r] sound* does not exists in Japanese. <u>Do not pronounce</u> りゃ, りゅ and りょ like (rya), (ryu), and (ryo). Listen to the video very carefully and practice the pronunciation.
    *The Spanish soft [r] sound is very close to Japnese [r] sound.

Part III: 36 Hiragana Characters with Semi-Vowel: [y]

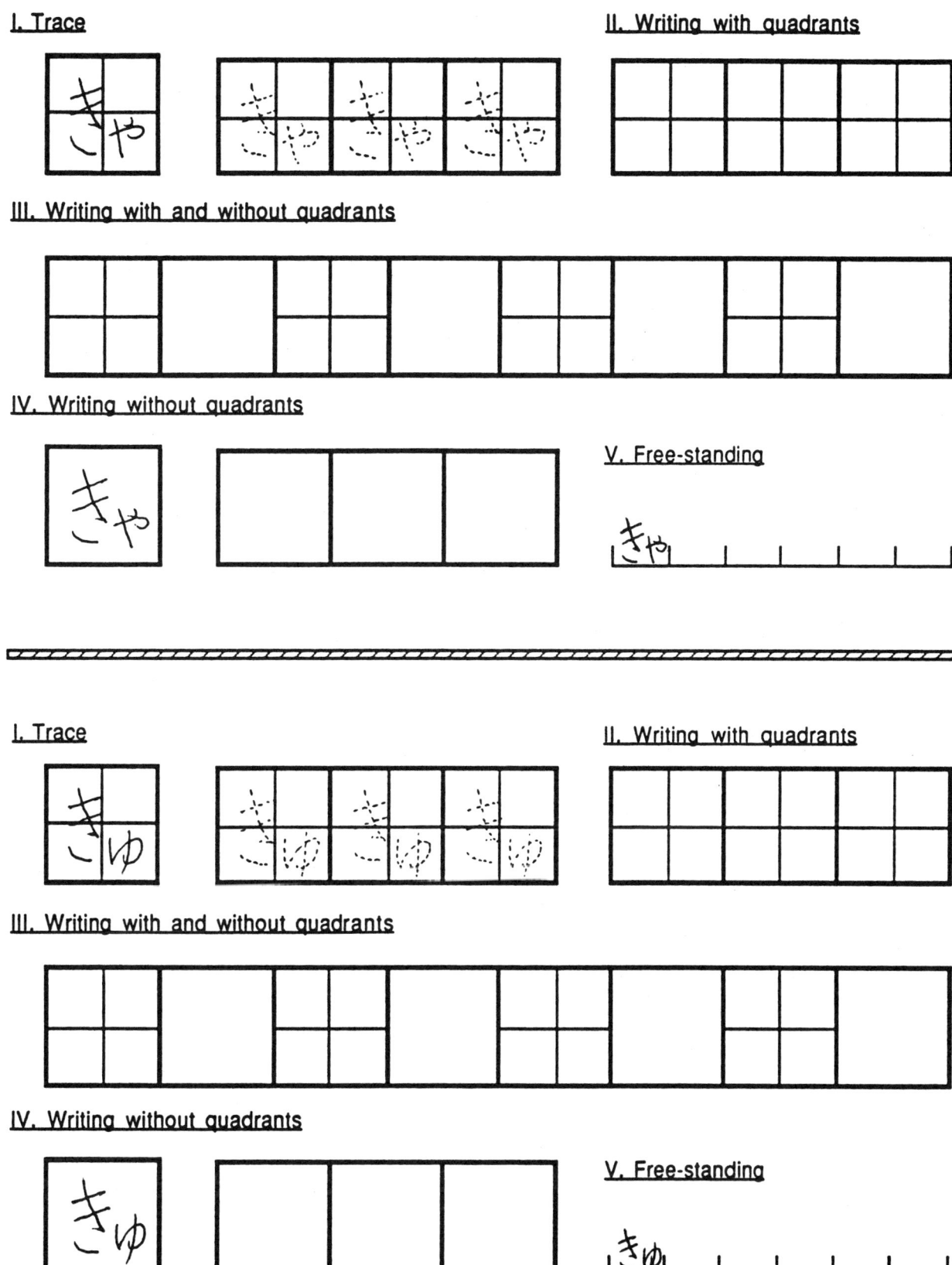

Part III: 36 Hiragana Characters with Semi-Vowel: [y]

I. Trace

II. Writing with quadrants

III. Writing with and without quadrants

IV. Writing without quadrants

V. Free-standing

きょ

I. Trace

II. Writing with quadrants

III. Writing with and without quadrants

IV. Writing without quadrants

V. Free-standing

ぎゃ

Part III: 36 Hiragana Characters with Semi-Vowel: [y]

78

I. Trace

II. Writing with quadrants

III. Writing with and without quadrants

IV. Writing without quadrants

V. Free-standing

ぎゅ

I. Trace

II. Writing with quadrants

III. Writing with and without quadrants

IV. Writing without quadrants

V. Free-standing

ぎょ

Part III: 36 Hiragana Characters with Semi-Vowel: [y]

I. Trace

しゃ

II. Writing with quadrants

III. Writing with and without quadrants

IV. Writing without quadrants

しゃ

V. Free-standing

しゃ

I. Trace

しゅ

II. Writing with quadrants

III. Writing with and without quadrants

IV. Writing without quadrants

しゅ

V. Free-standing

しゅ

Part III: 36 Hiragana Characters with Semi-Vowel: [y]

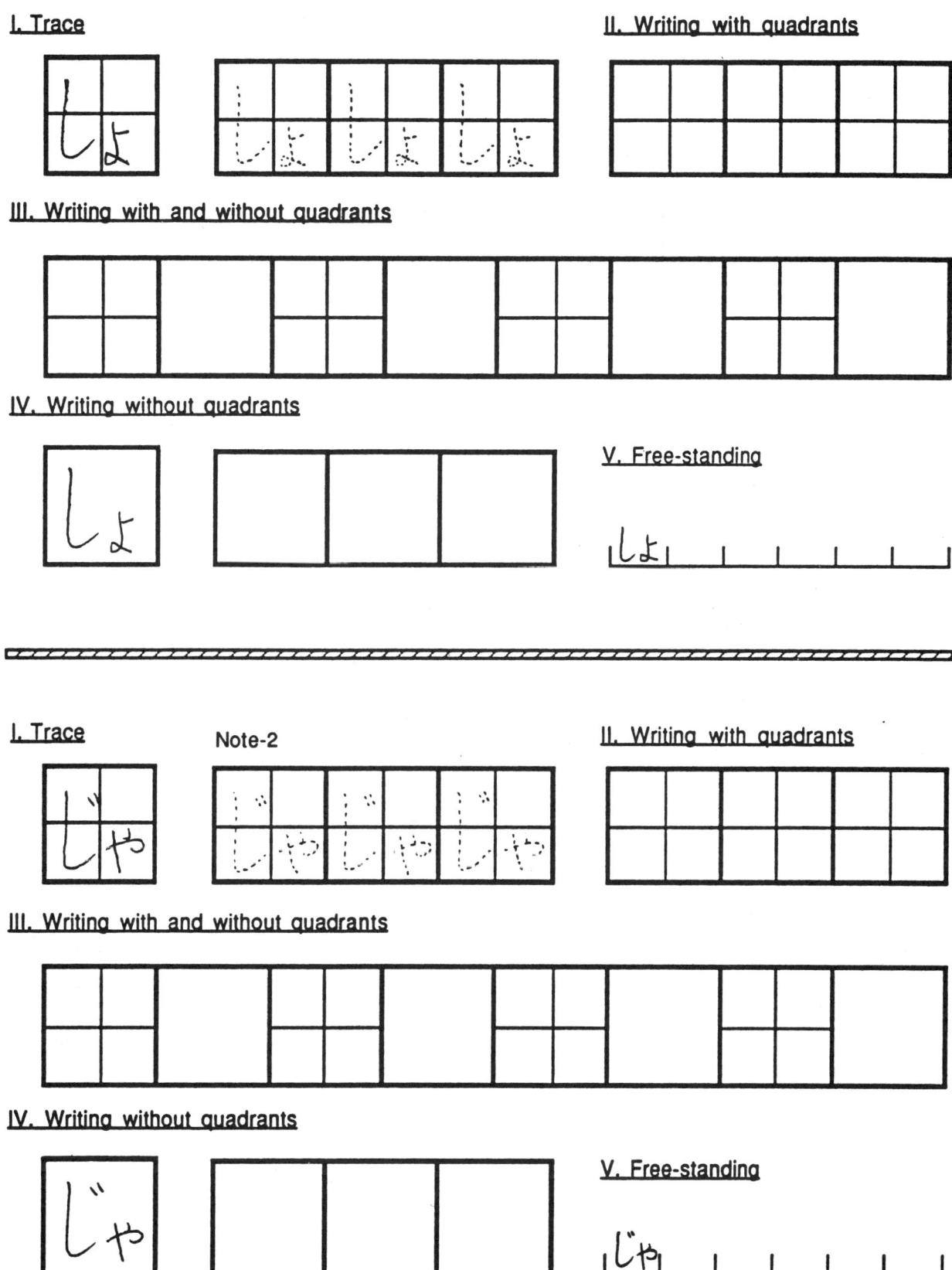

Part III: 36 Hiragana Characters with Semi-Vowel: [y]

I. Trace
じゅ

Note-2
じゅ じゅ じゅ

II. Writing with quadrants

III. Writing with and without quadrants

IV. Writing without quadrants
じゅ

V. Free-standing
じゅ

I. Trace
じょ

Note-2
じょ じょ じょ

II. Writing with quadrants

III. Writing with and without quadrants

IV. Writing without quadrants
じょ

V. Free-standing
じょ

Part III: 36 Hiragana Characters with Semi-Vowel: [y]

I. Trace

ちゃ

II. Writing with quadrants

III. Writing with and without quadrants

IV. Writing without quadrants

ちゃ

V. Free-standing

ちゃ

I. Trace

ちゅ

II. Writing with quadrants

III. Writing with and without quadrants

IV. Writing without quadrants

ちゅ

V. Free-standing

ちゅ

Part III: 36 Hiragana Characters with Semi-Vowel: [y]

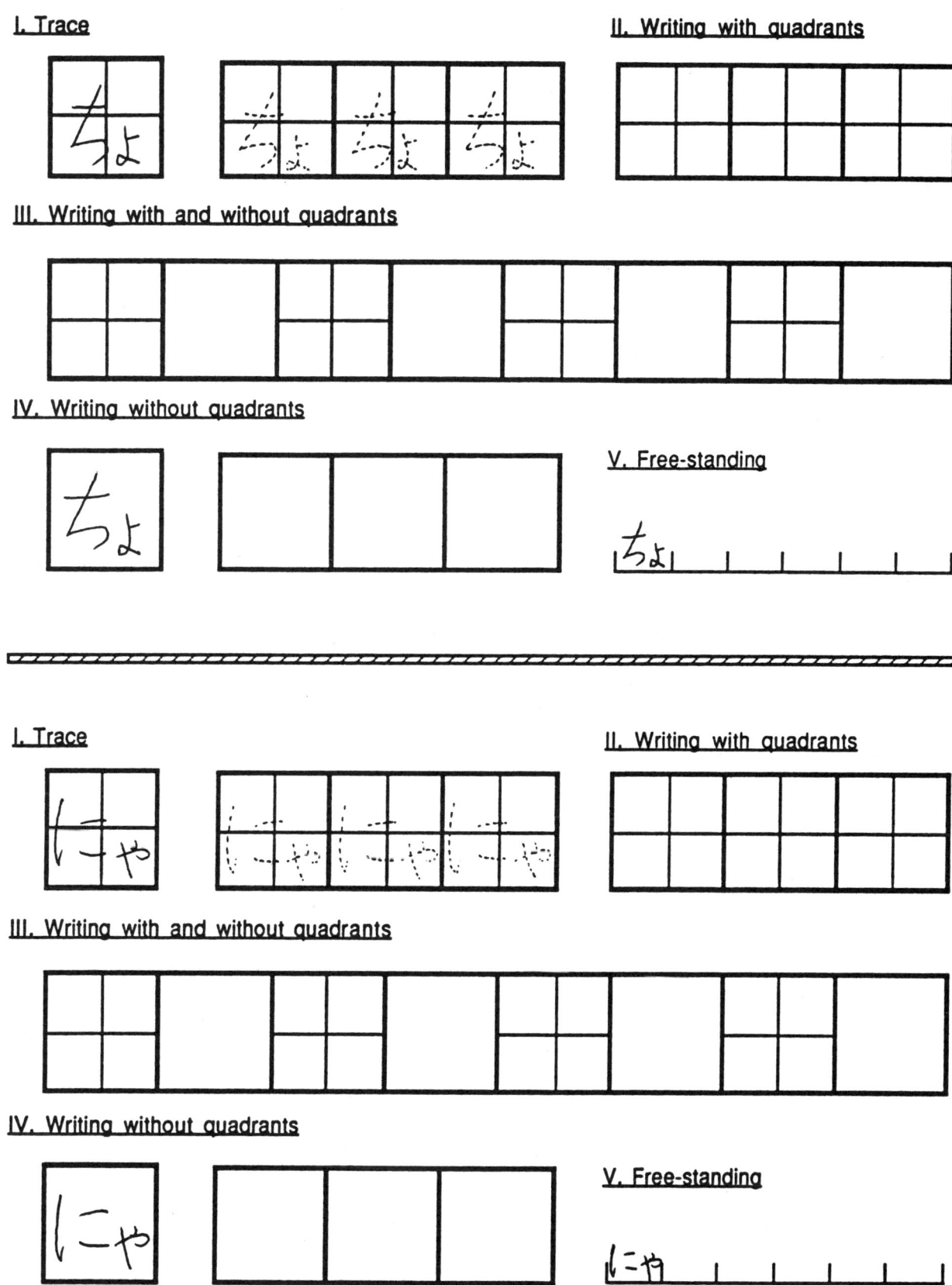

Part III: 36 Hiragana Characters with Semi-Vowel: [y]

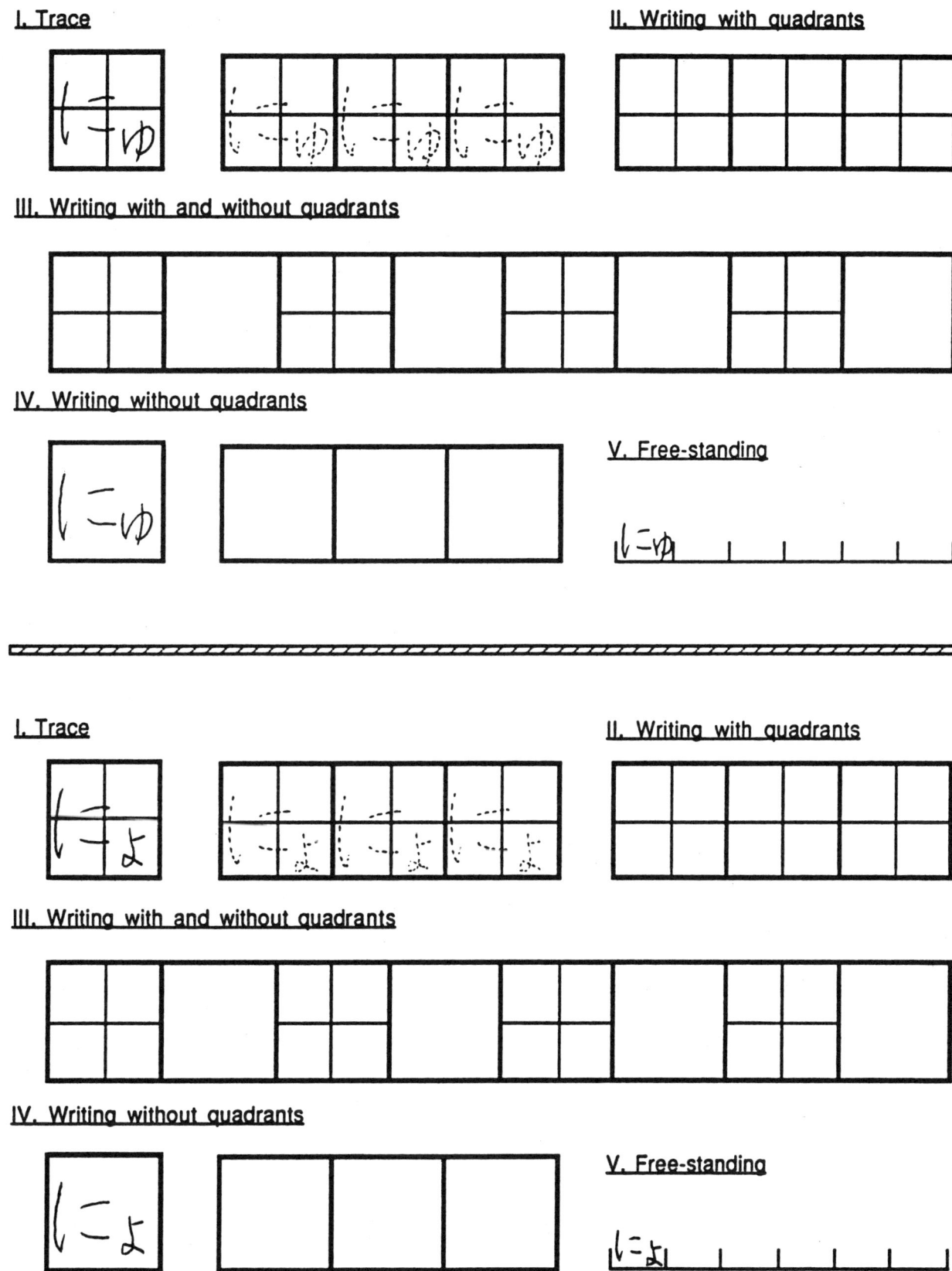

Part III: 36 Hiragana Characters with Semi-Vowel: [y]

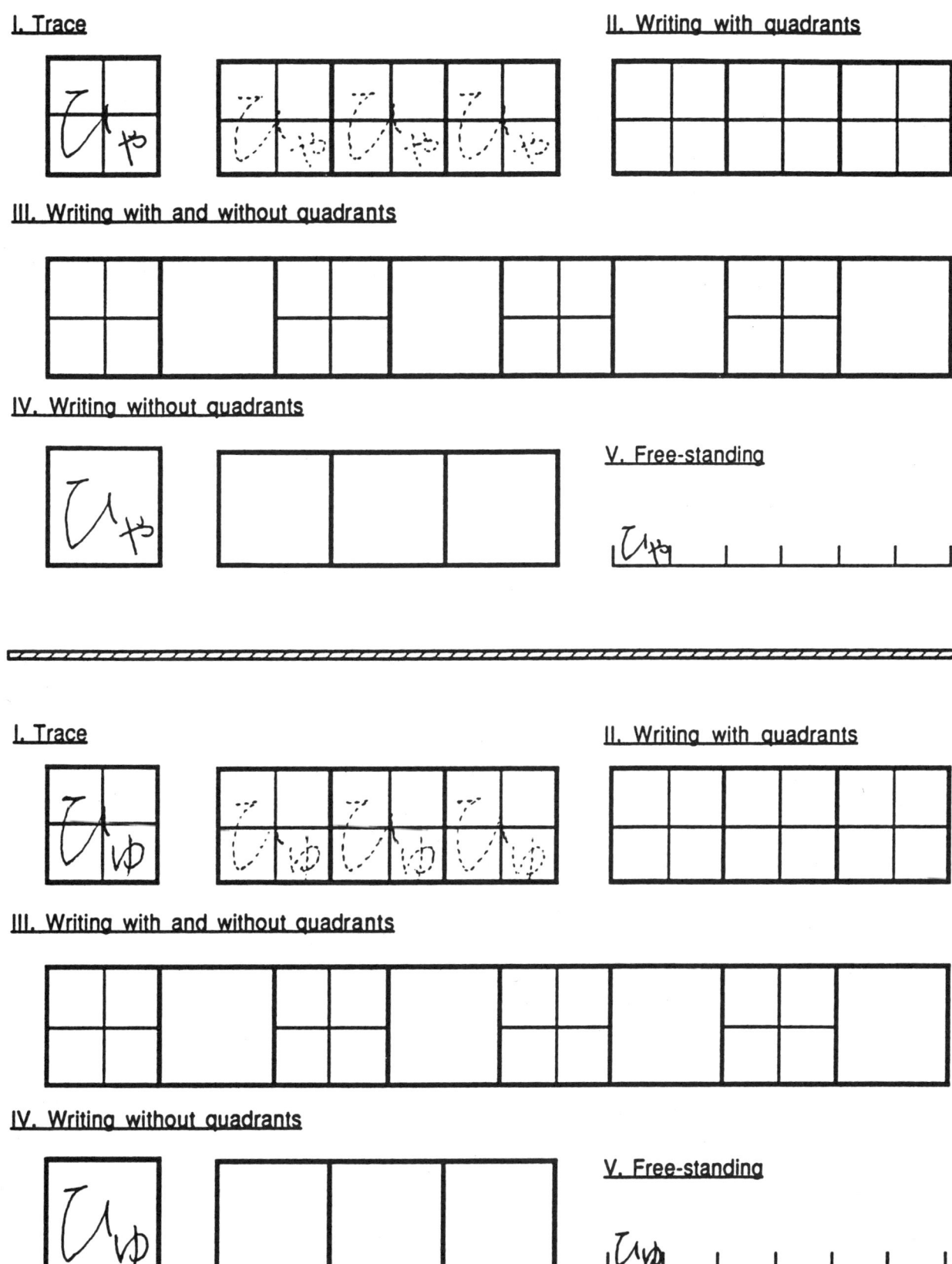

Part III: 36 Hiragana Characters with Semi-Vowel: [y]

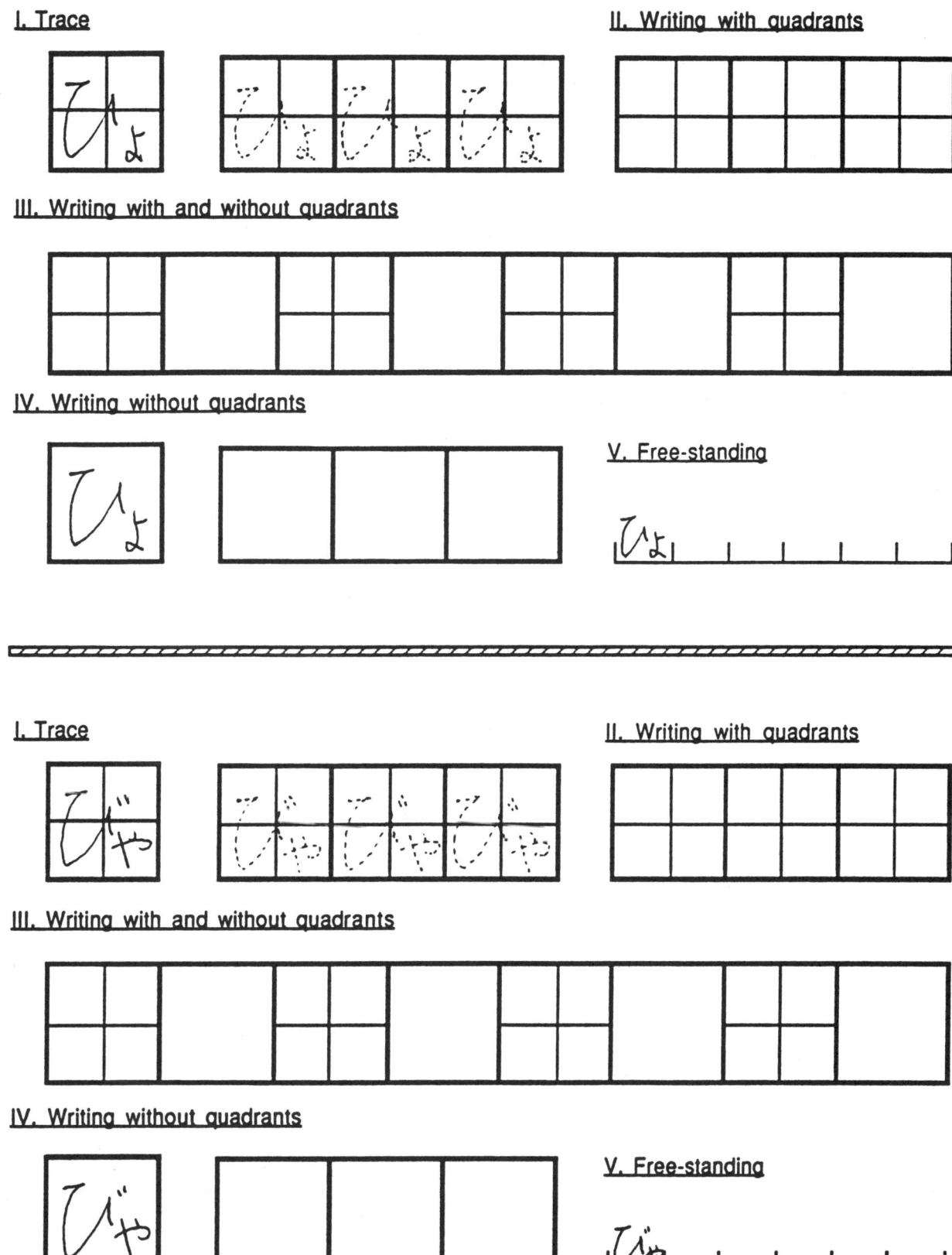

Part III: 36 Hiragana Characters with Semi-Vowel: [y]

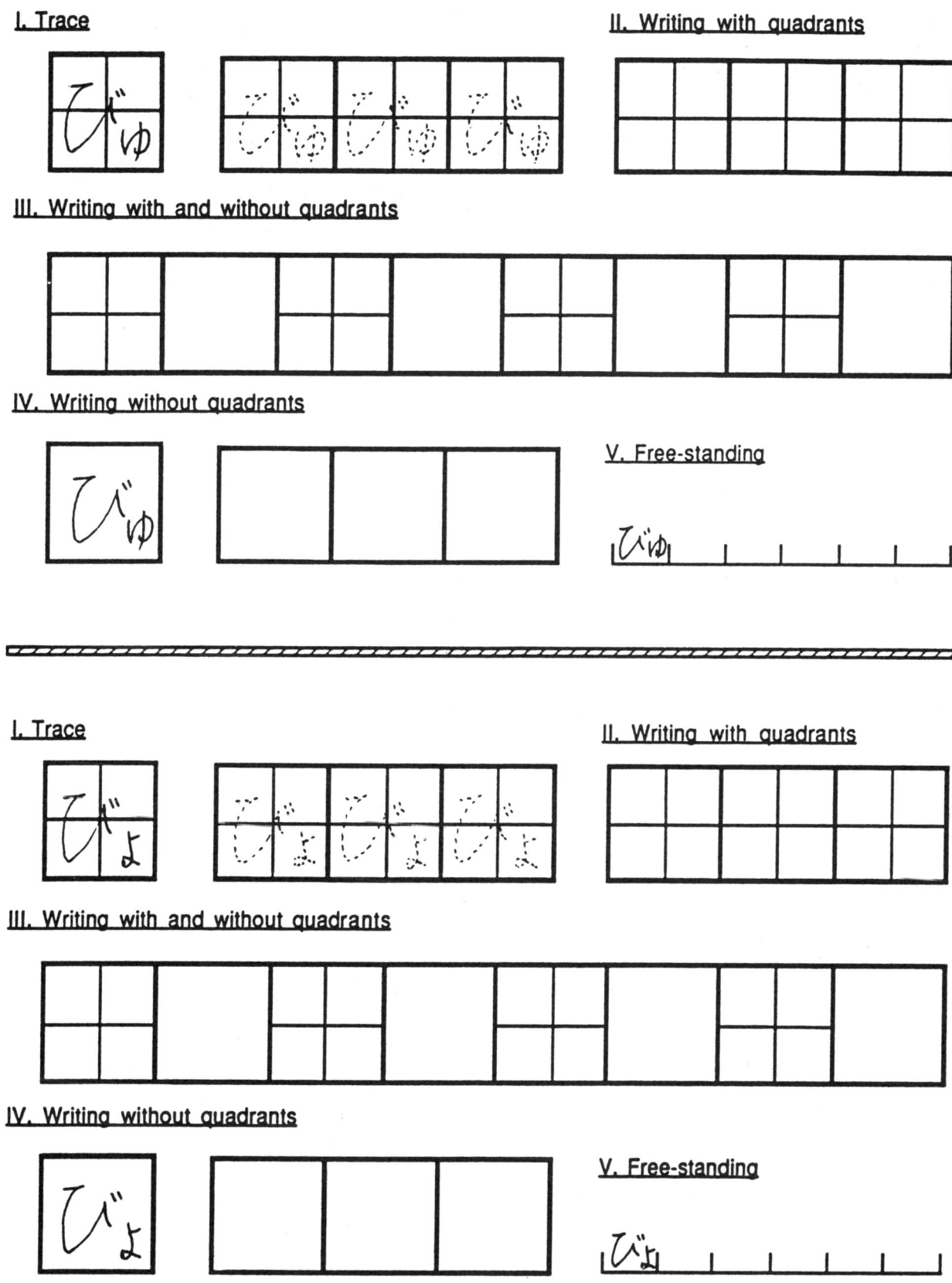

Part III: 36 Hiragana Characters with Semi-Vowel: [y]

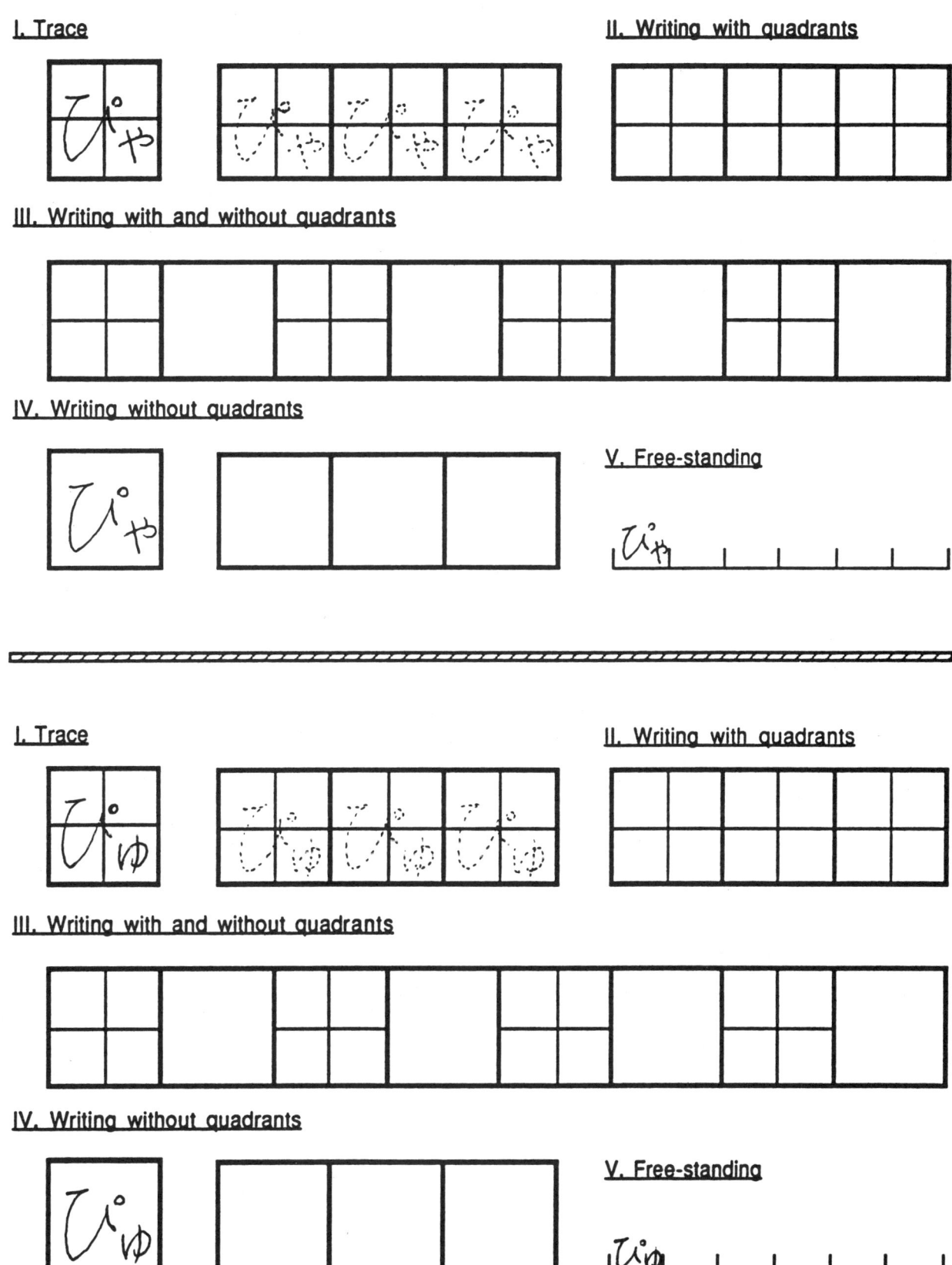

Part III: 36 Hiragana Characters with Semi-Vowel: [y]

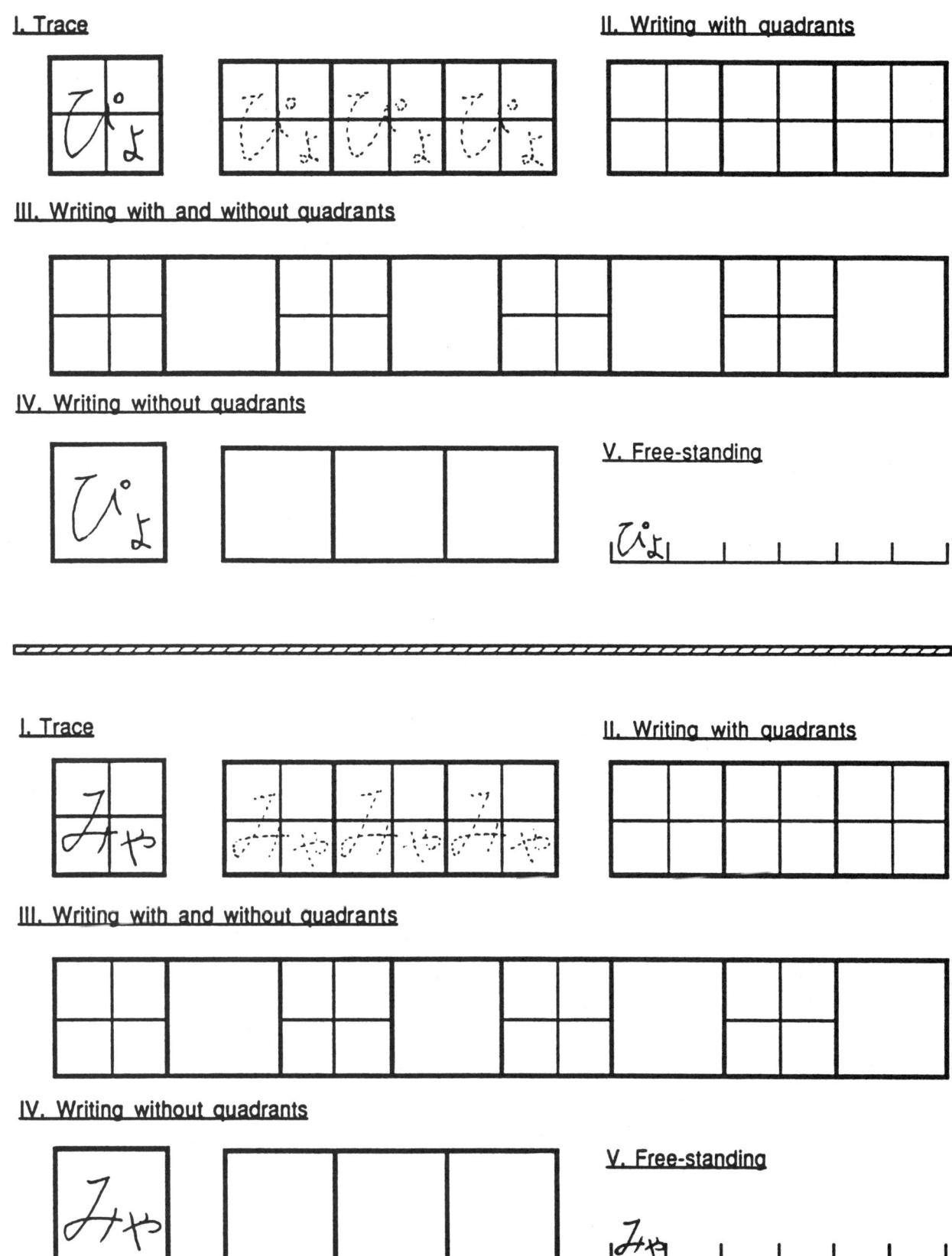

Part III: 36 Hiragana Characters with Semi-Vowel: [y]

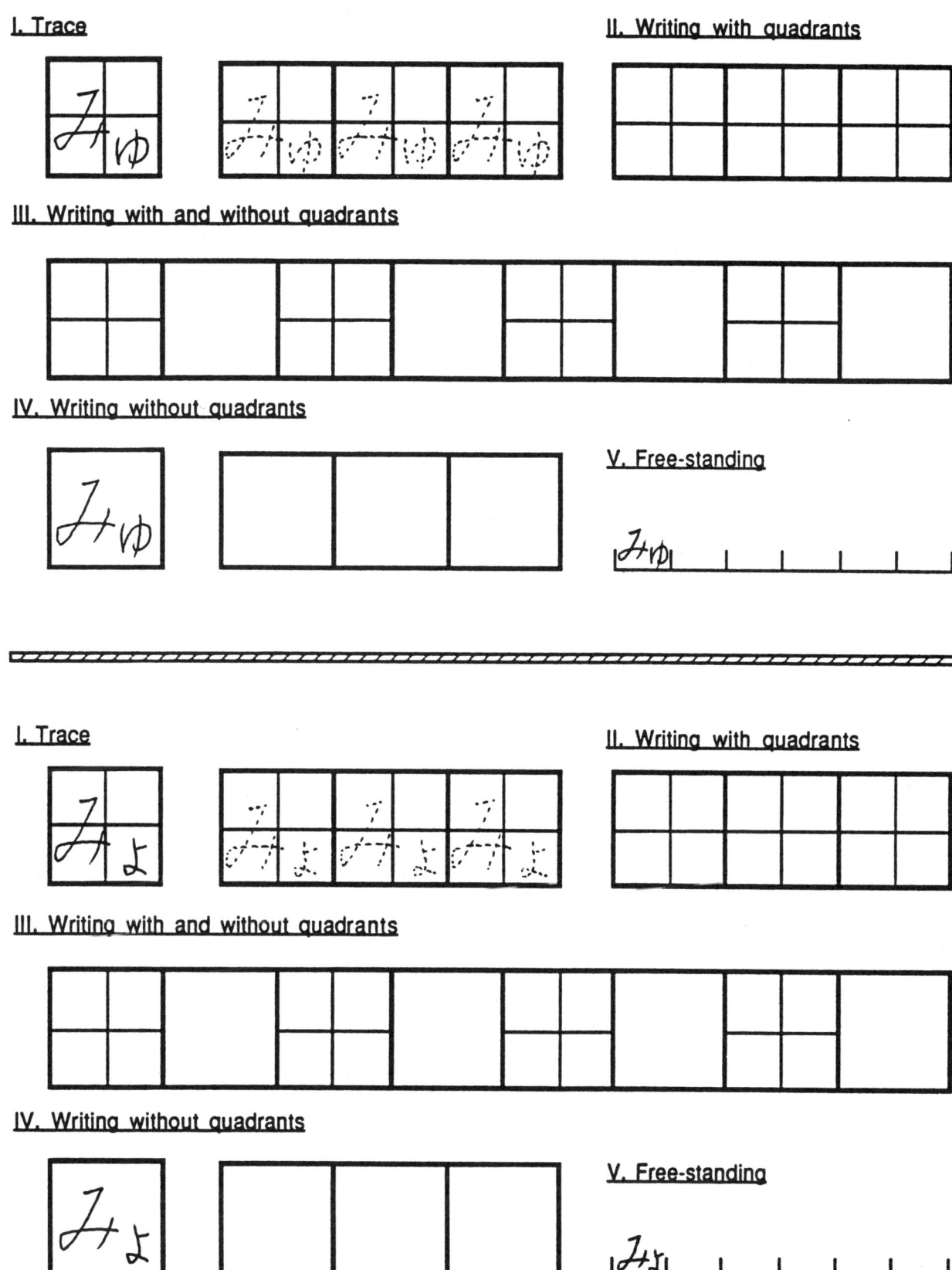

Part III: 36 Hiragana Characters with Semi-Vowel: [y]

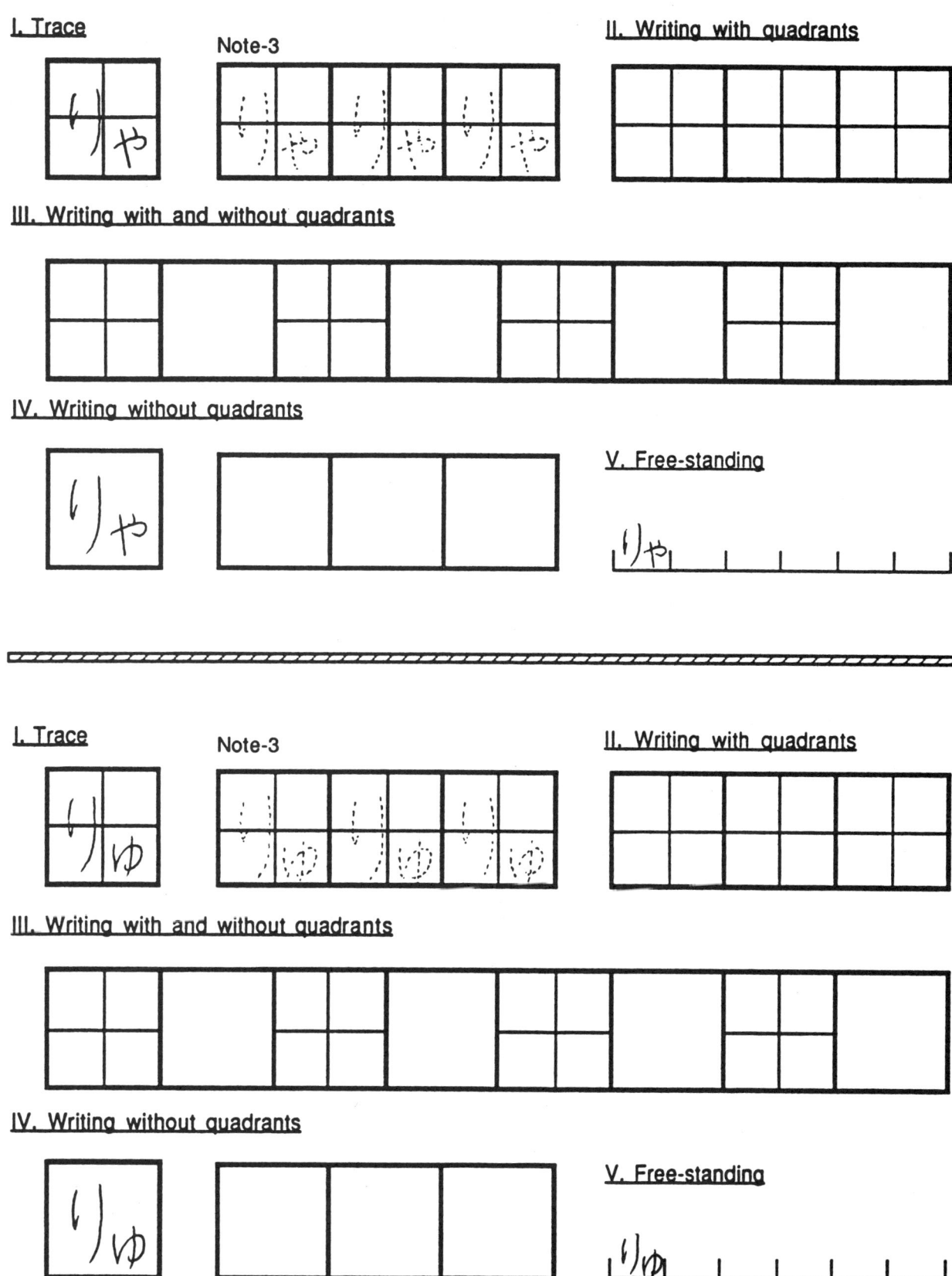

Part III: 36 Hiragana Characters with Semi-Vowel: [y]

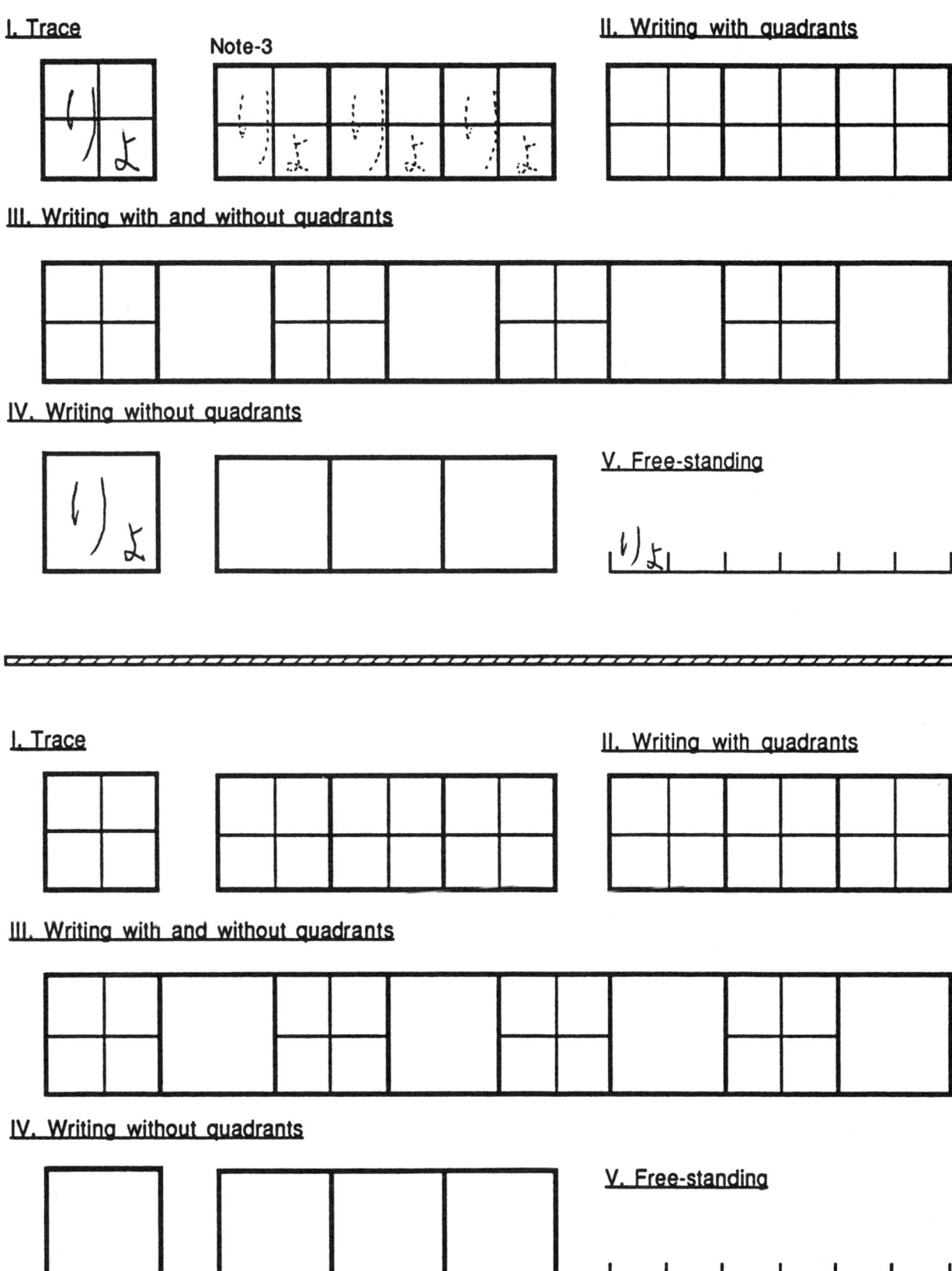

Part III: 36 Hiragana Characters with Semi-Vowel: [y]

Exercises
Correct answers are presented in APPENDIX A. The characters used in the following exercises may be slightly different from the ones you practiced; however, both are perfectly correct.

Exercise A:
On the video, 10 characters are shown. Pronounce each character and check if you have pronounced it correctly. Answers will be given immediately following the question on the video. Hence, answers for this exercise are not given in APPENDIX A.

Exercise B:
On the video, 15 Hiragana characters are pronounced. Find the characters in the chart below. Answer by indicating the number-letter combination which corresponds with the correct character.

Example: If きゃ is pronounced, answer 4-A because きゃ is found at the cross point between 4 and A in the chart below.

	A	B	C	D
1.	ぎゃ	しょ	ひゃ	にょ
2.	ぴゅ	きょ	りょ	じゅ
3.	じょ	ひゅ	しゃ	ぴょ
4.	きゃ	みゅ	ちゅ	びょ
5.	りゅ	にゅ	ひょ	りゃ
6.	ぎょ	ちゃ	じゃ	ぢゅ
7.	びゃ	しゅ	びゅ	にゃ
8.	みょ	ぎゅ	きゅ	みゃ
9.	ぢょ	ぢゃ	ぴゃ	ちょ

Answer here:

1. _____   6. _____   11. _____
2. _____   7. _____   12. _____
3. _____   8. _____   13. _____
4. _____   9. _____   14. _____
5. _____   10. _____   15. _____

Continue this exercise with your instructor and fellow students or a Japanese friend.

Part III: 36 Hiragana Characters with Semi-Vowel: [y]

Exercise C:
On the video, a Japanese word is pronounced. Find the word in the list of words below. Choose the word and answer with the letter assigned to the left of the word.

1. a. しやくしょ　　b. じゆうな　　c. しゅうにゅう　　d. じゅうなな

2. a. びょういん　　b. ちょういん　　c. にゅういん　　d. びよういん

3. a. じんじゃ　　b. しゃしん　　c. しゃいん　　d. しんじゅ

4. a. りょかん　　b. きょうかん　　c. ようかん　　d. りゅうかん

5. a. きょうし　　b. きゅうす　　c. ぎょうじ　　d. きょうじゅ

Continue this exercise with your instructor and fellow students or a Japanese friend.

Exercise D:
On the video, a Japanese word is pronounced. Write the word in Hiragana below. Each space is for one character.

1. ____ ____ ____ ____
2. ____ ____ ____ ____
3. ____ ____ ____
4. ____ ____ ____ ____
5. ____ ____ ____
6. ____ ____ ____
7. ____ ____
8. ____ ____
9. ____ ____ ____
10. ____ ____ ____ ____ ____
11. ____ ____ ____ ____
12. ____ ____ ____
13. ____ ____ ____
14. ____ ____ ____
15. ____ ____ ____

APPENDICES

APPENDIX A

List of Exercise Answers

PART I

Exercise A: Check with the video.

Exercise B:
1. 5-A
2. 9-E
3. 8-C
4. 2-C
5. 6-E
6. 3-E
7. 7-B
8. 1-D
9. 5-D
10. 7-D
11. 8-C
12. 2-D
13. 4-A
14. 6-B
15. 3-B

Exercise C: 1. c   2. a   3. d   4. b   5. c

Exercise D:
1. あき (autumn)
2. ねこ (cat)
3. さんすう (mathematics)
4. おとこ (a male)
5. むら (village)
6. かもめ (sea gull)
7. いけ (pond)
8. にほん (Japan)
9. やま (mountain)
10. つくえ (desk)
11. みち (road)
12. はる (spring season)
13. きって (postage stamp)
14. なわ (rope)
15. ゆめ (a dream)

PART II

Exercise A: Check with the video.

Exercise B:
1. 4-D
2. 1-A
3. 2-A
4. 5-E
5. 4-E
6. 3-E
7. 2-C
8. 3-D
9. 5-D
10. 2-D
11. 4-B
12. 2-E
13. 5-A
14. 1-C
15. 3-B

Exercise C: 1. d   2. b   3. a   4. c   5. a

Appendices

Exercise D:
1. ぎんこう (bank=financial institution)
2. だいがく (university)
3. せいざ (formal sitting position)
4. ちず (map)
5. ぼんさい (bonsai tree)
6. どうぞ (please.)
7. ごぜん (a.m.=ante meridiem)
8. がっこう (school)
9. かぶき (Kabuki theater)
10. じじつ (fact)
11. さんぽ (a walk)
12. げっこう (moonlight)
13. ばら (a rose)
14. でぐち (an exit)
15. きっぷ (ticket)

PART III

Exercise A: Check with the video.

Exercise B:
1. 4-C
2. 9-D
3. 8-A
4. 3-D
5. 6-B
6. 4-B
7. 8-C
8. 1-D
9. 5-D
10. 1-A
11. 5-B
12. 2-A
13. 7-A
14. 3-B
15. 2-C

Exercise C: 1. b   2. a   3. c   4. a   5. d

Exercise D:
1. じどうしゃ (car)
2. りゅうこう (trend)
3. こうちゃ (English tea)
4. ぎゅうにゅう (milk)
5. しちょう (mayor)
6. びょうき (sickness)
7. みゃく (pulse)
8. ひゃく (hundred)
9. じょうし (higher official)
10. とっきゅう (express train)
11. いっぴょう (one vote)
12. しょうが (ginger)
13. にんじゃ (ninja)
14. りょこう (trip)
15. じゅきょう (Confucianism)

APPENDIX B

List of Vocabulary Words

PART-I
Notes on Usage and Pronunciation

うみ	ocean
うさぎ	rabbit
うち	house
とうきょう	Tokyo
がっこう	school
きょう	today
もと	origin
よか	leisure time
がか	artistic painter
もっと	more
よっか	4th day of a month
がっか	academic subject
ぜんぶ	all
かんむり	crown
しんぱい	anxiety
こんど	this time
おんな	a female
かんたん	simplicity
ぎんざ	Ginza
げんかい	limitation
おんがく	music

Exercise C

はち	bee, number eight
たな	shelf
はな	flower
わた	cotton
ねむい	sleepy
くもり	cloudy
めくる	to turn (pages)
ぬるい	lukewarm
ほし	star
うし	cattle
はし	bridge, chop stick
けし	poppy plant
たき	waterfall
あさ	morning
かさ	umbrella
ゆき	snow
こい	carp, love
ここ	this place
もり	forest
かに	crab

Exercise D

あき	autumn
ねこ	cat
さんすう	mathematics
おとこ	a male
むら	village
かもめ	sea gull
いけ	pond
にほん	Japan
やま	mountain
つくえ	desk
みち	road
はる	spring (season)
きって	postage stamp
なわ	rope
ゆめ	a dream

PART-II
Exercise C

ざっし	magazine
ぶっし	goods
じっし	enforcement
ばっし	tooth extraction, suture removal
かんじ	Kanji characters
でんぶ	buttocks
じぶん	myself
こんぶ	edible sea kelp
ぎん	silver
びん	bottle
がん	cancer
だん	step
はっぷん	eight minutes
えんぴつ	pencil
しゅっぱん	publication

(Part -II, Exercise C, Cont')

うっかり	carelessly		きょうかん	instructor
ちがい	difference		ようかん	sweet jelly of beans
ごかい	a misunderstanding		りゅうかん	influenza
にがい	bitter		きょうし	educator
にかい	second floor		きゅうす	teapot

Exercise D

			ぎょうじ	event
			きょうじゅ	professor
ぎんこう	bank (financial institution)			
だいがく	university			
せいざ	formal sitting position			
ちず	map			
ぼんさい	bonsai tree			
どうぞ	please			
ごぜん	a.m. (ante meridiem)			
がっこう	school			
かぶき	Kabuki theater			
じじつ	fact			
さんぽ	a walk			
げっこう	moonlight			
ばら	rose			
でぐち	an exit			
きっぷ	ticket			

Exercise D

じどうしゃ	car
りゅうこう	trend
こうちゃ	English tea
ぎゅうにゅう	milk
しちょう	mayor
びょうき	sickness
みゃく	pulse
ひゃく	hundred
じょうし	higher official
とっきゅう	express train
いっぴょう	one vote
しょうが	ginger
にんじゃ	ninja
りょこう	trip
じゅきょう	confucianism

PART-III

Exercise C

しゃくしょ	city hall
じゆうな	free, unconfined
しゅうにゅう	income, revenure
じゅうなな	seventeen
びょういん	hospital
ちょういん	signature
にゅういん	hospitalization
びよういん	beauty shop
じんじゃ	shrine
しゃしん	photograph
しゃいん	company employee
しんじゅ	pearl
りょかん	traditional Japanese inn

APPENDIX C

List of All Hiragana Characters

PART I: 46 Basic Hiragana Characters

	a	i	u	e	o
1.	あ	い	う	え	お
2.	か	き	く	け	こ
3.	さ	し	す	せ	そ
4.	た	ち	つ	て	と
5.	な	に	ぬ	ね	の
6.	は	ひ	ふ	へ	ほ
7.	ま	み	む	め	も
8.	や		ゆ		よ
9.	ら	り	る	れ	ろ
10.	わ				を
11.	ん				

PART II: 25 Hiragana Characters with Consonants: [g, z, d, j, b, p]

1.	が	ぎ	ぐ	げ	ご
2.	ざ	じ	ず	ぜ	ぞ
3.	だ	ぢ	づ	で	ど
4.	ば	び	ぶ	べ	ぼ
5.	ぱ	ぴ	ぷ	ぺ	ぽ

PART III: 36 Hiragana Characters with Semi-Vowel: [y]

1.	きゃ	きゅ	きょ
2.	ぎゃ	ぎゅ	ぎょ
3.	しゃ	しゅ	しょ
4.	じゃ	じゅ	じょ
5.	ちゃ	ちゅ	ちょ
6.	ぢゃ	ぢゅ	ぢょ
7.	にゃ	にゅ	にょ
8.	ひゃ	ひゅ	ひょ
9.	びゃ	びゅ	びょ
10.	ぴゃ	ぴゅ	ぴょ
11.	みゃ	みゅ	みょ
12.	りゃ	りゅ	りょ